# MONEY
# AND CAPITAL
## *in Economic Development*

RONALD I. McKINNON

# MONEY
# AND CAPITAL
*in Economic Development*

THE BROOKINGS INSTITUTION
*Washington, D.C.*

338.09
M 158

*Library of Congress Cataloging in Publication Data:*

McKinnon, Ronald I
   Money and capital in economic development.

   Includes bibliographical references.
   1. Economic development   2. Finance.   3. Capital.
I. Title.
HD82.M334    338'.09    72-9928
ISBN 0-8157-5614-3
ISBN 0-8157-5613-5  (pbk.)

*9 8 7 6 5 4 3 2 1*

THE BROOKINGS INSTITUTION is an independent organization devoted to nonpartisan research, education, and publication in economics, government, foreign policy, and the social sciences generally. Its principal purposes are to aid in the development of sound public policies and to promote public understanding of issues of national importance.

The Institution was founded on December 8, 1927, to merge the activities of the Institute for Government Research, founded in 1916, the Institute of Economics, founded in 1922, and the Robert Brookings Graduate School of Economics and Government, founded in 1924.

The Board of Trustees is responsible for the general administration of the Institution, while the immediate direction of the policies, program, and staff is vested in the President, assisted by an advisory committee of the officers and staff. The by-laws of the Institution state, "It is the function of the Trustees to make possible the conduct of scientific research, and publication, under the most favorable conditions, and to safeguard the independence of the research staff in the pursuit of their studies and in the publication of the results of such studies. It is not part of their function to determine, control, or influence the conduct of particular investigations or the conclusions reached."

The President bears final responsibility for the decision to publish a manuscript as a Brookings book or staff paper. In reaching his judgment on the competence, accuracy, and objectivity of each study, the President is advised by the director of the appropriate research program and weighs the views of a panel of expert outside readers who report to him in confidence on the quality of the work. Publication of a work signifies that it is deemed to be a competent treatment worthy of public consideration; such publication does not imply endorsement of conclusions or recommendations contained in the study.

The Institution maintains its position of neutrality on issues of public policy in order to safeguard the intellectual freedom of the staff. Hence interpretations or conclusions in Brookings publications should be understood to be solely those of the author or authors and should not be attributed to the Institution, to its trustees, officers, or other staff members, or to the organizations that support its research.

# Foreword

STRATEGIES for the economic development of poor countries traditionally have emphasized large foreign aid transfers, capital inflows, or disguised subsidies from industrialized nations. But these forms of assistance are in some cases insufficient to overcome the recipients' fundamental economic problems, and in others they may actually be damaging. After a quarter-century of foreign aid, it appears that much of the effort has yielded disappointing results.

Theoretical analyses of development also emphasize the lack of resources, such as physical capital, managerial capacity, and other "real" factors, to the almost complete exclusion of financial factors other than foreign exchange limitations on the capacity to import. In this study, Ronald I. McKinnon charts a different approach to the development problem. Instead of emphasizing the scarcity of capital, he focuses on the extraordinary distortions commonly found in the domestic capital markets of developing countries.

His analysis leads to a critique of existing monetary theory and to a new view of the relation between money and physical capital in developing countries. He finds that the impact of monetary and financial policies on their capital markets is much greater than is generally supposed, and that their governments often follow policies that stifle incentives to save and invest. Repression of the financial sector is paralleled by the use of tariffs and quotas in an effort to promote development by manipulating the foreign trade sector.

Mr. McKinnon advances theoretical arguments and empirical evidence to suggest that a more effective strategy for economic growth would proceed from a thorough liberalization of financial markets and the lifting of restraints on foreign trade. He points out that several countries have followed such a "bootstrap" strategy, aimed at securing their own economic development without having to rely on foreign aid and foreign capital investment. Why liberalization of financial markets is necessary and how to achieve it without incurring undue social and economic costs are the principal concerns of this book.

A professor of economics at Stanford University and a member of Brookings' associated staff, Mr. McKinnon completed this study in 1970–71 on leave from Stanford as the Rockefeller Visiting Research Professor at Brookings. His analytical viewpoint owes much to Emile Despres and Edward Shaw, his colleagues at Stanford, who encouraged his interest in developing countries and in the financial approach to economic development. He is grateful to both, though neither might agree fully with his views.

Mr. McKinnon also acknowledges the contribution of Walter S. Salant, whose suggestions regarding technical economic issues are reflected throughout the study. Others who read the manuscript and made valuable comments are Richard N. Cooper, Harry G. Johnson, and Lawrence B. Krause. Peter T. Knight, Hayne Leland, and John Scadding provided helpful advice on specific problems.

Margaret McKinnon gave extensive editorial assistance and much needed encouragement. At Brookings, Evelyn P. Fisher checked the data for accuracy, Virginia C. Haaga edited the final manuscript, and Joan C. Culver prepared the index.

The views expressed in the study are, of course, solely those of the author and should not be ascribed to the trustees, officers, or other staff members of the Brookings Institution.

KERMIT GORDON
*President*

*October 1972*
*Washington, D.C.*

# Contents

## Tables

# *Figures*

# 1

# Introduction

CAN ONE EXPLAIN why economic wealth is high or rising in a fairly pervasive way in some countries, while other countries languish? Extraordinary differences among nations in cultural heritage, natural resources, colonial experience, and political structure seem to defy any purely economic analysis. Various authors have tried to identify necessary historical stages in the development process. Others have advocated particular policies, such as the "import substitution" strategy of industrialization, based on mathematical planning or programming techniques. By and large, such views have been found wanting both in empirical explanation and as guides to policy. None would have predicted the accentuation of economic disparity between rich industrial nations and most poor countries in the postwar years—a singularly distressing fact, which E. H. Phelps Brown has associated with the "underdevelopment of economics."[1] Nevertheless, the problem continues to attract sophists and calculators because it is so important.

Even the most intrepid, however, must narrow his scope with respect to time and place and in selecting policy issues to be examined. My concern is primarily, although not exclusively, with what are now called "less developed countries"—LDCs—and their experience from the end of the Second World War to the present

1. E. H. Phelps Brown, "The Underdevelopment of Economics," *Economic Journal,* Vol. 82 (March 1972), pp. 1–10.

1

time. Can one use a single frame of reference to explain why Japan has done better than India, Mexico better than Colombia, and Taiwan better than the Philippines? The analysis focuses on semi-industrial LDCs—those that have made more or less autonomous efforts to industrialize or to develop some commercial agriculture, perhaps with the help of capital inflows from abroad or foreign technical assistance. Brazil, Chile, Pakistan, and Turkey will be covered more directly than will the pristine economies of Africa. Socialist economies will be included insofar as they use prices to allocate resources in commodity and factor markets.

The approach is heavily "bootstrap" in emphasis. As long as potential access to international trade remains remarkably free, as it has in the postwar period, successful development rests mainly on policy choices made by national authorities in the developing countries. Correspondingly the inadequate economic performance of many LDCs is attributed to repressive, though understandable, economic policies that they themselves have pursued. Indeed, the role of international capital transfers—by government-to-government aid or by private multinational corporations—is regarded as less important than it is conventionally assumed to be and is analyzed only cursorily in the last chapter of this book. Similarly the approach implicitly de-emphasizes, by ignoring, such topics of current interest as tariff preferences for LDC exports to wealthy countries, the formation of customs unions among groups of poor countries, and the establishment of more elaborate international cartels (commodity agreements) for governing trade in primary products.

The centerpiece of the theory is the *domestic* capital market within each developing country and the way in which that market's operations are influenced by monetary and fiscal policies. Money and finance, as governed largely by the banking system, are given a degree of importance much greater than that accorded by most authors concerned with development. For convincing me of the importance of financial processes, I shall always be indebted to my colleague, Edward Shaw, of Stanford University. The remarkable financial transformation that occurred in 1965–66 in Korea—where Shaw was an influential adviser—has provided great intellectual stimulation for undertaking a more general investigation of monetary policies in successful and in lagging economies. The statistical evidence indicates that the Korean case is not as unique as it first appeared to me when I began this research. Whether authorities decided to nourish and expand the "real" stock of money (that is, the stock of money measured by its value in relation to the prices of goods and services) or allowed it to remain shrunken and heavily taxed, has critically affected the relation between saving and income and the efficiency of investment in a number of countries, as is demonstrated empirically in Chapter 8.

The need for something more than additional statistical evidence soon became apparent, however. Accepted theories of monetary and financial processes—whether they be Keynesian or monetarist—cannot explain the dominance of real money balances in the operation of capital markets in poor countries. Both of these prevailing theories assume that capital markets are essentially "perfect," with a single governing rate of interest or a term structure of interest rates, whereas the brute fact of underdevelopment is overwhelming fragmentation in real rates of interest. As a result, both theories treat real money balances and physical capital as substitutes for each other, although a relation of "complementarity" better explains the data in certain critical circumstances.

Hence, an alternative monetary model is developed in Chapters 6 through 9. Although this new theoretical approach lacks the completeness and elegance of either short-run Keynesian theory or the "long-run" monetary growth models now in vogue, its basic assumptions are better suited to explaining the relationship between monetary processes and capital accumulation in the underdeveloped world. Important issues of inflation versus deflation, higher or lower rates of interest, growth or stagnation depend on which theoretical viewpoint is adopted. I hope that this formulation of the problem for LDCs is also relevant for mature economies that face monetary difficulties.

Once the monetary linchpin is put in place, appropriate strategies for liberalizing foreign trade and rationalizing domestic tax and expenditure policy follow naturally. Indeed, a certain critical mutuality exists where fiscal policies are needed to support the release of monetary restraint and vice versa. Successful liberalization of the domestic capital market permits a radical restructuring of tariff, quota, and licensing restraints on foreign trade; whereas a correct policy toward the foreign exchange rate is necessary to secure control over the money supply.

The need for more "outward looking" foreign trade policies for most developing countries is now generally accepted within the economics profession. More controversial is the nature of an efficient liberalization strategy. The postwar history of LDCs is replete with attempts to liberalize foreign trade—frequently with substantial aid from the International Monetary Fund or other consortia of international lenders from wealthy countries. Nevertheless, few such liberalizations have been sustained, and regression back to more repressive tariffs and exchange controls is commonplace.

Two views are prevalent about liberalization of the constricted foreign trade sector. One is that liberalization, interpreted mainly as the removal of import controls and tariffs, should be gradual, covering first "essential" producer and consumer goods and last "inessential" consumer items; and that protection should be removed first from domestic industries that are mature enough to withstand international competition and last from infant industries. The second view is that foreign aid or other external credits should come with the liberalization of foreign trade. Their purpose is to provide external financing for the increased imports that removal of controls seems to portend. Assistance from abroad has been considered useful and even necessary in helping to liberalize the economy over the critical and possibly painful adjustment period.

These views are plausible. Unfortunately, they may well be wrong, as is shown in Chapter 11. Complete rather than partial liberalization is more likely to be ultimately successful. Somewhat more surprisingly perhaps, the absorption of substantial amounts of foreign capital during the liberalization process may also be a serious mistake. That is, it may be easier to remove protective tariffs and quotas on foreign trade by *avoiding* extraordinary capital inflows from abroad. Such unconventional wisdom is, of course, in accordance with my optimistic view that most poor countries can secure their own successful development.

# 2

## Capital in a Fragmented Economy

WHILE ECONOMISTS CAN usefully divide their labor as monetary theorists, tax experts, foreign trade specialists, project evaluators, and so on, a unified view of the development process is a great analytical convenience. Why is public intervention so pervasive and generally so unsuccessful? Intervention is usually prompted by the perception—sometimes correct—that a particular market is functioning badly, so that authorities feel pressed to "do something." An infant textile firm is helped by a tariff; or the price of an agricultural product may be raised to permit farmers to use a new fertilizer-intensive technology; or a tax exemption may be granted to a foreign firm for automobile assembly. This pressure for public intervention is the result of severe fragmentation in the underdeveloped economy.

### The Fragmented Economy

The economy is "fragmented" in the sense that firms and households are so isolated that they face different effective prices for land, labor, capital, and produced commodities and do not have access to the same technologies. Authorities then cannot presume that socially profitable investment opportunities will be taken up by the private sector, because prevailing prices need not reflect true economic scarcity—at least not for large segments of the population. There is historical justification for this view in the nineteenth and early twentieth centuries. In Asia, Latin America, and Africa, primary commodity export enclaves were controlled by foreigners, and much of the general population remained outside of the market economy. Indigenous entrepreneurs had limited access to capital, no means of acquiring advanced technologies, and little skilled labor.

> Thus in the determination of where in the vast new areas of the overseas world the raw material export industries were to be established, the pre-existing domestic supply of labor, capital, and entrepreneurship played a minimal role. Where they did exist in areas of potential export production, these factors were highly immobile and could not be counted upon to engage in export industry operation.[1]

Newly independent governments quite properly felt compelled to act as agents of change to offset economic and political colonialism. In the past twenty or thirty years, poor countries have succeeded in introducing some new industrial activities—particularly the manufacture of goods previously imported—and in mobilizing some domestic factors of production. Their governments chose to do so, however, by manipulating commodity prices in a variety of ways and by intervening directly to help some individuals or sectors of the economy at the expense of others.

Consider the extraordinary lengths to which import tariffs have been used in Latin America (see Table 10-1), with rates of several hundred percent on some goods and absolute prohibitions on the import of others, while still others enter freely. The situation on the Indian subcontinent is no different. Price and quantity controls on foreign trade and domestic commerce make licensing and rationing commonplace. Byzantine patterns of industrial taxes and subsidies complicate government budgetmaking. Consequently,

---

1. Jonathan V. Levin, *The Export Economies: Their Pattern of Development in Historical Perspective* (Harvard University Press, 1960), p. 169. For a good description of how small farmers, who are strongly motivated toward economic efficiency, can nonetheless be locked into a backward agricultural technology, see Theodore W. Schultz, *Transforming Traditional Agriculture* (Yale University Press, 1964), pp. 36–48.

the market mechanism has become no better, and perhaps even worse, as an indicator of social advantage.

Modern fragmentation, therefore, has been largely the result of government policy and goes beyond the old distinction between the export enclave and the traditional subsistence sector. One manifestation is the often-noted existence of small household enterprises and large corporate firms—all producing similar products with different factor proportions and very different levels of technological efficiency. Continuing mechanization on farms and in factories in the presence of heavy rural and urban unemployment is another. Excess plant and equipment with underutilized capacity are commonly found in economies that are reputed to be short of capital and that do suffer from specific bottlenecks. In rural areas, tiny landholdings may be split up into small noncontiguous parcels, with inadequate incentives for agricultural land improvements.[2]

While tangible land and capital are badly used, fragmentation in the growth and use of human capital can be more serious and no less visible. Learning-by-doing and on-the-job training in the "organized" economy are confined to narrow enclaves—export-oriented in the past but now increasingly inward-oriented toward "modern" manufacturing—whose employment growth may be less than the growth in general population.[3] Unemployment among the highly educated coexists with severe shortages in some labor skills.

Indigenous entrepreneurship is narrowly based and is supported by heavy government subsidy. Tariff protection, import licenses, tax concessions, and low-cost bank finance commonly go to small urban elites and create great income inequality between the wealthy few and the poverty-stricken many. This income inequality has failed to induce high rates of saving in the classical manner, but governments remain reluctant to reduce the disposable income

2. See, for example, the Indian case analyzed by B. S. Minhas in "Rural Poverty, Land Redistribution and Development Strategy: Facts and Policy" (International Bank for Reconstruction and Development, Economic Development Institute, September 1970; processed).

3. See David Turnham assisted by Ingelies Jaeger, *The Employment Problem in Less Developed Countries: A Review of Evidence* (Paris: Development Centre of the Organisation for Economic Co-operation and Development, 1971), p. 94.

of well-to-do investors whose unique access to investment opportunities is guaranteed by the web of official controls and by the endemic fragmentation.

## *Liberalization and the Capital Market*

How does one begin to loosen the Gordian knot? The incredibly complex distortions in commodity prices now prevailing are the unplanned macroeconomic outcome of specific microeconomic interventions. But substantial fragmentation in the markets for land, labor, and capital provided the initial motivation for public authorities to "do something" and continues to pressure governments to intervene. Thus an explicit policy for improving the operation of factor markets is necessary to persuade authorities to cease intervening in commodity markets. Carefully considered liberalization in all sectors can then move forward—not merely as a reaction to the more obvious mistakes of the immediate past, but in ways that allay legitimate fears of pure laissez-faire.

However, the knot needs to be loosened further. To say that there are "imperfections in factor markets" is distressingly vague and often signals the end of formal economic analysis. But further systematic inquiry can proceed if the neoclassical approach of treating labor, land, and capital symmetrically as primary factors is dropped. It is hypothesized here that fragmentation in the capital market—endemic in the underdeveloped environment without carefully considered public policy—causes the misuse of labor and land, suppresses entrepreneurial development, and condemns important sectors of the economy to inferior technologies. Thus appropriate policy in the domestic capital market is the key to general liberalization, and particularly to the withdrawal of unwise public intervention from commodity markets.

Efficient capital markets, however, pose subtle questions of economic and social organization that go far beyond the provision of physical infrastructure. The accumulation of capital per se means little in the underdeveloped economy, where rates of return on some physical and financial assets are negative while extremely remunerative investment opportunities are forgone. One farmer may save by hoarding rice inventories, part of which is eaten by mice so that the return on his saving is negative. Another may foresee an annual return of over 60 percent in drilling a new tube well for irrigation, but the local moneylender wants 100 percent interest on any loan he provides. The operator of a small domestic machine shop may find it impossible to get bank credit to finance his inventories of finished goods and accounts receivable, whereas an exclusively licensed importer of competitive machine parts has easy access to foreign trade credit at a subsidized rate of 6 percent.

In the face of great discrepancies in rates of return, it is a serious mistake to consider development as simply the accumulation of homogeneous capital of uniform productivity. This simplistic view has been held explicitly by economic growth theorists and econometricians who incorporate homogeneous capital of uniform productivity into production functions. It is held implicitly by policymakers in less developed countries (LDCs), who all too often have followed a strategy of maximizing short-run gross investment in virtually any form. It has been abetted by official international agencies that calculate the "need" for foreign aid on the assumption that output–capital ratios in recipient countries are fixed.

It seems important to develop a distinct alternative view of the role of capital. To focus the analysis still more narrowly, let us define "economic development" as the reduction of the great dispersion in social rates of return to existing and new investments under domestic entrepreneurial control. The capital market in a "developed" economy successfully monitors the efficiency with which the existing capital stock is deployed by pushing returns on physical and financial assets toward equality, thereby significantly increasing the average return. Economic development so defined is necessary and sufficient to generate high rates of saving and investment (accurately reflecting social and private time preference), the adoption of best-practice technologies, and learning-by-doing.

The converse is not likely to be true, however. Arbitrary measures to introduce modern technology via tariffs, or to increase the rate of capital accumulation by relying on foreign aid or domestic forced saving, will not necessarily lead to economic development. Thus it is hypothesized that unification of the capital market, which sharply increases rates of return to domestic savers by widening exploitable investment opportunities, is essential for eliminating other forms of fragmentation.

### Production Opportunities, Wealth, and External Finance: A Fisherian Approach

How can one succinctly characterize the fragmented state of the capital market in the underdeveloped economy? First, income categories are not well defined, nor are the processes of saving and investment specialized, as they would be in advanced economies. With a large, self-financed household or "unorganized" sector and an imperfectly financed corporate or "organized" sector, there is little use in emphasizing a class structure that is based on the functional distribution of income among wages, profits, interest, and land rents. Nor is much gained from sharply distinguishing a saving class from an investing class, and both from a laboring class. Rather, there are many entrepreneurs who provide labor, make technical decisions, consume, save, and invest. The term "entrepreneur" will be used henceforth to denote individuals or families performing all five functions; and a model of entrepreneurial behavior that is characteristic of much indigenous rural and urban economic life is established.

Capital theory involves decision making over time in a fundamental way. The model presented here is built around Irving Fisher's[4] approach to impatience and intertemporal choice, as extended and elaborated by Jack Hirshleifer.[5] Neither of these valuable treatises has been applied specifically to the development problem as it is defined here, but they provide a convenient framework for viewing the way in which the capital constraint impinges on the decision making of entrepreneurs.

The scope for intertemporal decision making, within which the entrepreneur maximizes his utility, can usefully be reduced to three components: (1) his endowment or owned deployable capital; (2) his own peculiar productive or investment opportunity; and (3) his market opportunities for external lending or borrowing over time outside his own enterprise. At a very general level, a fragmented capital market, which is characteristic of underdevelopment, is one where the three components are badly correlated. That is, entrepreneurs with potential production opportunities

4. Irving Fisher, *The Theory of Interest* (Macmillan, 1930).
5. J. Hirshleifer, *Investment, Interest, and Capital* (Prentice-Hall, 1970).

lack resources of their own, as well as access to external financing. Those with substantial endowments may lack "internal" production opportunities (unless such opportunities are artificially generated by public intervention) and have no "external" investment outlets at rates of return that accurately reflect the prevailing scarcity of capital. The resulting dispersion in real rates of return reflects the misallocation of existing capital and represses new accumulation.

The Fisherian approach is distinctive because it does emphasize the individuality of each entrepreneur, who has his own more or less unique production opportunity. This opportunity depends on his specialized knowledge (technical expertise being very scarce and differentially distributed) and the factors of production available to him—family labor, landholdings, structures, and so on. Whether a man is a good farmer, a sophisticated carpenter and builder, or an efficient retailer determines his production possibilities and his need for investment in human and physical capital to exploit them. There is tremendous diversity in skills and talent throughout the rural and urban populations, but they are attached to small firm–households and not easily identified.

Correspondingly there is no single authority or narrow class of individuals who can extract saving and allocate investment according to a neoclassical menu of best-practice production techniques. Unlike the situation in highly developed economies, there are few if any great indigenous agglomerations of capital under the control of organizations with proven technical expertise. Endowments do not necessarily correspond to opportunity. Thus there is but a fine line between the efficient division of labor and uneconomic fragmentation.

What can pull the fragments together so that the efficient division of labor prevails? Since one cannot rely on initial endowments to supply capital, supplemental financing from outside the individual enterprise is of critical importance in determining whether or not high-productivity investments are undertaken. It is more critical in poor economies that are trying to break out of past patterns of using capital than in wealthy ones with established investment and reinvestment patterns. The aggregate consumable surplus or "capital" available to all LDC entrepreneurs at any one point in time must be reshuffled among them somehow so that those with the best internal opportunities are net recipients of funds, even though some of these recipients may be net suppliers of funds in later periods, all on a *quid pro quo* basis. Then small but highly productive individual investments in seed-fertilizer packages, on-the-job labor training, equipment purchases, or inventory holding can all be encompassed by a single allocative mechanism. The need for "public" decision making in each sphere of economic activity is correspondingly reduced.

Unfortunately, financing from outside the individual enterprise is either unavailable or extremely limited in the underdeveloped environment. Raymond W. Goldsmith[6] has shown statistically that newly issued primary securities are a much smaller proportion of gross national product (GNP) and of aggregate saving in underdeveloped countries than in wealthy ones. The extent of intermediation through the banking system is also relatively limited, as will be shown below.

In Chapter 3, specific public policies affecting both industry and agriculture are interpreted as responses to this constraint on external finance. First, however, the problem in the absence of compensating public intervention is examined.


## *Indivisible Investments and Technological Innovation*

Superimposed on our Fisherian model of fragmented investment opportunities is the problem of "indivisibilities." Typically, investments associated with the adoption of markedly improved technologies bulk large in the eyes of small-scale entrepreneurs. Investing in an improved breed of dairy cattle, buying a simple lathe or sewing machine, or assembling a new combination of seeds, fertilizers, and pesticides necessarily require quantum changes in cash outlays from a net income that may be barely sustaining the entrepreneur and his family. Poverty and the inability to borrow to finance *discrete* increases in expenditures can be formidable barriers to the adoption of even the simplest and most productive innovations.

Indeed, without indivisibilities, self-financed capital accumulation—where saving and investment take place within the same

6. *Financial Structure and Development* (Yale University Press, 1969), p. 374.

firm—might well be sufficient for a slow diffusion of new technologies and a gradual reduction in the dispersion in rates of return within and between various enterprises. Marginal innovative investments by poor but thrifty entrepreneurs would thrive, because divisible investments could be financed directly by marginal reductions in current consumption. With indivisibilities so important in practice, however, financially isolated entrepreneurs can easily be caught in a low-level equilibrium trap, where innovation is completely blocked except for a small handful of the very wealthy, who get wealthier. Discrepancies in earned rates of return may actually increase.

Although limited to self-finance, the "typical" entrepreneur can still make certain important investment and consumption decisions that serve to allocate his capital over time. Within the confines of traditional technology applied to his own enterprise, he can choose to consume marginally less now and more later—that is, to invest a consumable surplus. For example, a farmer can decide to leave some of his land fallow, at the cost of a smaller crop this year, in order to get a larger one next year. With an unsophisticated agricultural technology, the internal return from deferring current consumption is likely to be quite low.

Now suppose that a "green revolution" has taken place and the farmer has succeeded in building up his working capital—seeds, pesticides, fertilizer—and his fixed capital—irrigation facilities—which put him on a whole new technology. The same kind of marginal balancing can take place in the context of this new technology. The farmer could provide his own savings to increase slightly the commercial fertilizer that he is now using, and the return on this marginal new investment could be calculated.

The important point, however, is the virtual impossibility of a poor farmer's financing from his current savings the whole of the balanced investment needed to adopt the new technology. Access to external financial resources is likely to be necessary over the one or two years when the change takes place. Without this access, the constraint of self-finance sharply biases investment strategy toward marginal variations within the traditional technology. This bias is demonstrated formally in the technical note at the end of this chapter, where the standard Fisherian diagram portraying intertemporal investment and consumption is modified to take account of the indivisibility that is associated with the introduction of a distinctly new technique.

This emphasis on external financial restraint is different from the dominant neoclassical theory of technological diffusion and "learning." The prevailing theory begins by assuming that there is a perfect capital market equalizing all private rates of return, that indivisibilities are not important, and that entrepreneurs have similar production opportunities. Evident frictions or imperfections in technological diffusion must then be explained differently by recourse to "external" or "extra-market" effects. Kenneth Arrow[7] has suggested that learning-by-doing in an *industry* depends on the level of gross investment undertaken by *individual firms*. Learning by one entrepreneur spills over or becomes more easily copied by others. To promote these social benefits not captured in individual decision making, Arrow concludes that a state subsidy to gross investment in high-learning industries is warranted.

A subsidy to gross investment in any particular industry, however, would be entirely inappropriate in a world where traditional technologies coexist with modern ones, and it is seldom clear to government authorities which of the two has the highest rate of return. Indeed, as will be discussed in Chapter 3, authorities in poor countries have subsidized investments in modern plant and machinery extensively, with highly perverse results. The internal rate of return that a particular enterprise can earn—which varies greatly by entrepreneur within and across industries—is a much better index of learning-by-doing than is some measure of gross investment. Fortunately, the internal rate of return itself can attract enough resources to individual firm–households if an adequate capital market exists. State subsidies to encourage technical innovation can then be confined to more general support for research and development and the dissemination of information through institutions like agricultural extension services.

## The Importance of High Rates of Interest

Is then the provision of cheap external finance to small-scale industry and agriculture the correct strategy for the government to follow? Notice that our small farmer, contemplating a discrete

7. Kenneth J. Arrow, "The Economic Implications of Learning by Doing," *Review of Economic Studies*, Vol. 29 (June 1962), pp. 155–73.

investment in the "green revolution," can greatly improve his position even if he has to borrow at a rate that *exceeds* the marginal rate of return under self-financed investments with the old technique.[8] Artificially low-cost loans or subsidized credit programs may be both unnecessary and unwise.

Consider the pooling of savings in a number of similarly situated, although not identical, firm–households. The borrowing rate for firms undertaking discrete investments can be closely related to the return seen by those who are net savers. By paying a rate of interest on financial assets that is significantly above the marginal efficiency of investment in existing techniques, one can induce some entrepreneurs to disinvest from inferior processes[9] to permit lending for investments in improved technology and increased scale in other enterprises. Even though all entrepreneurs will continue to do some internal investing, a higher proportion of gross savings will pass through the external capital market. The release of resources from inferior uses in the underdeveloped environment is as important as new net saving per se.

The enterprise with the most productive investment possibility can change from one point in time to the next. That is, once one firm or farm upgrades its technology, the repayment flow can then be used by another to do the same—again at a sufficiently high rate of interest to lure funds away from lower-yield investments elsewhere. Given different productive opportunities across family firms, no single firm need continually outbid others that also have possibilities for modernization. Rather, one can imagine a sequence of discrete investments by different entrepreneurs as new technologies become diffused throughout the economy.

Where loans are plentiful, high rates of interest for both lenders and borrowers introduce the dynamism that one wants in development, calling forth new net saving and diverting investment from inferior uses so as to encourage technical improvement. In contrast, the common policy of maintaining low or negative rates of interest on financial assets and limited loan availability may accomplish neither. It is easy for authorities to underestimate the possible yield from loans to small-scale enterprises that have low re-

8. This possibility is demonstrated more formally in the technical note at the end of this chapter, where the slope of $T_1T_1'$ at $B$ in Figure 2-1 is exceeded by the slope of $CD$, the borrowing rate.

9. As illustrated by the movement from $B$ to $E$ in Figure 2-1, below.

turns on existing investments. By comparison, established enclaves in export, or import-substitution, industries may seem more lucrative because of their historically freer access to domestic and foreign sources of external finance. However, evidence is provided in Chapter 7 that potential returns to the efficient deployment of finance in the indigenous economy can be much higher than in the established enclaves.

## Uncertainty and Leverage

The disadvantages of capital accumulation through self-finance have been discussed at some length. But what prevents the development of financial institutions that break the confines of self-finance? The answer is, of course, *uncertainty,* which fragments the interest rate structure so that it no longer uniformly reflects the community's collective time preference. "The effect of risk . . . is to lower the rate of interest on safe loans, though at the same time . . . it will raise the rate of interest on unsafe loans. . . ."[10] In addition, "the necessity of having to offer collateral will affect not only the rate which a man has to pay, but the amount he can borrow. It will limit therefore the extent to which he can modify his income stream by this means."[11]

Many unfortunate public policies are attempts to get around the uncertainty that plagues capital markets in underdeveloped economies, as is specifically illustrated in Chapter 3. Financial institutions for reducing uncertainty at some cost in real resources are explored in Chapters 6 through 8. The remainder of this chapter is limited to two objectives: (1) to characterize briefly the inadequacies of current approaches to the pure theory of uncertainty, and (2) to distill a point of view more relevant for the development problem as defined here.

In contrast to the fragmentation hypothesis, prevailing theories of uncertainty assume that individual savers and investors are quite free to select whatever portfolios of physical and financial assets they choose. Moreover, to do so they can borrow—issue their

10. Fisher, *The Theory of Interest,* p. 218.
11. *Ibid.,* pp. 210–11.

own liabilities—without restraint at a given rate of interest. This freedom characterizes the "mean-variance" approach to uncertainty, associated with James Tobin[12] and the "state-preference" approach of Kenneth J. Arrow.[13]

In this theoretical context, uncertainty can be defined "objectively" in terms of the variable returns one might experience in holding alternative physical and financial assets. This variability in expected rates of return is the same for all asset holders or "entrepreneurs," although wealth owners may differ in their personal willingness to assume risk. The principal *raison d'être* of the financial system, then, is to ensure that risk-bearing is distributed according to people's "taste" for risk-taking. Risk averters will hold safe assets with lower yields. Those with a taste for risk will hold high-variance, high-return assets and may borrow or leverage themselves to do so. Indeed, "potential private borrowers are individuals with little or no risk aversion."[14]

In the underdeveloped world, however, neither individuals nor the government have a common menu of physical assets, with objectively defined probability distributions of rates of return. Indeed, if the division of labor is at all important, investment and production opportunities will be highly differentiated—even among government departments. The efficiency with which different assets are operated will depend on who owns or manages them. Consequently, the best investment opportunities (those with the highest expected rate of return) need not be the most risky, defined in the objective sense. Entrepreneurs (potential borrowers) in a position to exploit these high-return opportunities may or may not be risk preferers. Nevertheless they are likely to be constrained from investing by their own limited wealth and inability to borrow.

Similarly, potential lenders (savers)—even those with a significant personal taste for risk bearing—may have limited internal

12. "Liquidity Preference as Behavior Towards Risk," *Review of Economic Studies*, Vol. 25 (February 1958), pp. 65–86, is the first of many articles in which Tobin has employed this approach.

13. "The Role of Securities in the Optimal Allocation of Risk-bearing," *Review of Economic Studies*, Vol. 31 (April 1964), pp. 91–96, is the seminal article, with the original French version appearing earlier.

14. James Tobin, "Notes on Optimal Monetary Growth," *Journal of Political Economy*, Vol. 76 (July/August 1968), Pt. 2, p. 854.

investment opportunities of their own, and no external outlet. For example, they may be farmers who are confined to low-yield saving-investment within a traditional technology. Over all, differences in production opportunities and information availability can be expected to swamp differences in personal taste for risk-bearing—with the latter the concern mainly of operators of gambling casinos. The potential increases in real output associated with an improved financial structure, therefore, are much greater than the conventional theory of uncertainty would have one believe.

Why "subjective" uncertainty exists among firm–households (potential lenders and borrowers) is easy enough to see. Economic units, on both the saving and the investing side, are small. Reliable information on any one contemplated loan or investment may be costly, relative to its size, for outsiders to obtain. Repayment records are not well established, and many units operate with little liquidity. The fear of bankruptcy or default—which hardly enters at all into conventional uncertainty theory—pervades the underdeveloped economy.

In dealing with this interpersonal uncertainty and imperfect information, *leverage* becomes a key consideration. Many entrepreneurs can obtain no significant leverage through borrowing and are limited to investing their initial endowments. Moreover, for those who can obtain some external financing, their initial endowments may be an important form of collateral to ensure good performance. Thus initial endowment and capacity to borrow are complementary over a significant range, and leverage is particularly limited for those with small endowments. Ideally, a highly developed capital market markedly reduces the correlation between initial wealth holding and access to external finance.

Uncertainty, which reduces leverage in the amount an entrepreneur can borrow, also shortens the time horizon over which he can borrow. Finance is at very short term in the underdeveloped economy, severely limiting the intertemporal redistribution of entrepreneurial resources. The same need for collateral or security is manifested in demand for a quick visible payoff on the trickle of external finance that is provided. Thus borrowing has a time dimension and a quantity dimension, both of which are severely limited. Contrary to prevailing theories, unlimited personal freedom to select asset portfolios does not exist.

Moderating uncertainty and reducing fragmentation in capital markets require careful monetary and financial policies and a benign view of institutions that facilitate borrowing and lending over time. This, however, has generally not been the route followed by authorities in LDCs where organized and unorganized finance have languished and/or been actively repressed. Rather, various devices are used to *substitute* for nonoperative capital markets, as will be seen. Implicitly, governments have been strongly influenced by the financial constraint, but have responded with various "second-best" policies that have turned out to have unfortunate consequences.

## Technical Note

The problem of allocating investment and consumption over time is telescoped into a two-period Fisherian diagram in Figure 2-1. Individuals may abstain from consumption (invest) in period one in order to augment their consumable output in period two. Income or starting wealth, $Y$, as well as consumption, $C$, in period one are measured on the horizontal axis. Investment in the first period increases the income flow in the second, which is measured on the vertical axis. Internal investment opportunities, initial endowments, and the possibilities for borrowing and lending externally can all be encompassed by the diagram.

To illustrate the problem of "indivisibilities," it has been assumed that internal investments within the firm can be made only in the context of two distinct technologies. $T_1T_1'$ is a "traditional" agricultural technology with continually diminishing returns to investment beginning at $T_1$. $T_1T_1'$ defines the farmer's trade-off between reducing consumption in period one in order to increase it in period two, without significant innovation in agricultural technique. In contrast, $T_2T_2'$ may represent a more mechanized technique or an irrigation system. There is a discontinuity in returns—associated with the purchase of the initial equipment or the building of an irrigation ditch—since an investment of $T_1T_2$ is

FIGURE 2-1. *The Relation of Investment to the Choice between Traditional and New Techniques*

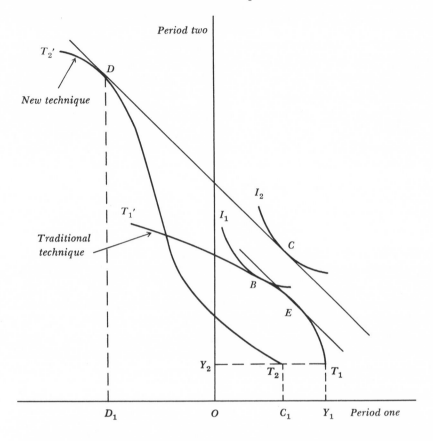

required before one can get *any* output from the second technique. Once this investment is made, however, returns to cultivation are very high and begin to diminish only as one moves along $T_2 T_2'$ well into the second quadrant.

$Y_1$ represents his beginning endowment, which consists of consumable capital carried over from the past and current income in period one. $Y_2$ can be interpreted as unimproved income accruing in period two if *no* investments were made in period one. Thus the level of current investment from the initial endowment is measured from $Y_1$ or $T_1$ to the left; and the slope of $T_1 T_2'$ gives the profitability of each dollar of current investment in increasing period two's consumable income.[15] The fact that the investment locus extends to the left into the second quadrant indicates simply that investment opportunities exceed the current endowment.

The limited initial endowment relative to consumption needs can bias the choice of technique if the entrepreneur is restricted to self-finance. First and second period consumption can be positive in a balanced fashion at *B* only when the enterprise uses the traditional technology; whereas first period consumption would have to be negative—an economic impossibility—if the economies of scale of the superior technique were effectively utilized. The consumption indifference curves for the entrepreneur/household are given the conventional convex shapes in $I_1$ and $I_2$. Consumption must be positive in both periods, and one can expect this consumption constraint to bind severely in poor economies. In the case portrayed in Figure 2-1, the consumption constraint and limited endowment lock the entrepreneur into an inferior technology at point *B*.

Access to external borrowing, however, will permit the entrepreneur to break out of the traditional mold with higher production, using new technology at *D* and with much improved consumption at *C*. That is, if he can borrow as much as he wishes at the rate of interest given by the slope of the straight line *DC*, this external finance will permit him to invest $Y_1 D_1$ in the new technology *and* increase consumption in period one. The gain in private and social productivity permits him to repay the loan in period two. Notice that the slope of *DC*, which defines the rate at which he can borrow, is greater than the marginal productivity of self-financed investment at point *B*, under the traditional technology.

In an idyllic "fully developed" economy, such intertemporal transactions would take place freely so that neither consumption limitations nor sparse initial endowment would inhibit high-return investments where "lumpiness" or indivisibilities were important. In short, poverty would be no barrier to the efficient deployment of the country's limited capital.

---

15. Since this two-period model is well established in the literature, the reader is referred to Hirshleifer, *Investment, Interest, and Capital*, especially Chaps. 2 and 3, for further clarification of the underlying concepts.

# 3

## The Intervention Syndrome

IN THIS CHAPTER, common public policies for circumventing the domestic capital market in industry and agriculture are first classified in seven major categories. Then their common biases and inefficiencies in dealing with unemployment, productivity growth, and income distribution are analyzed and linked to prevailing fiscal theories of "second-best" optimization.

*1. Tariff Protection for Infant Industries.* Ministers of trade and industry are deluged with plausible allegations that particular new industries or firms need protection to cover initial losses, although they will ultimately be profitable at world prices. A "temporary" tariff or quota restriction on competing imports raises the internal price of the domestic output at little immediate political cost. The cash flow or endowment available to the new industry is then increased while it is in the learning stage. This is the principal technique for implementing the import substitution strategy common to almost all underdeveloped economies. It has been recognized as such by the General Agreement on Tariffs and Trade (GATT), which provides that developing countries can raise such tariffs freely, under Article 18, without threat of reciprocal restrictions by advanced industrial nations.

As Harry G. Johnson[1] and others have pointed out, however, an

1. "Optimal Trade Intervention in the Presence of Domestic Distortions," in Robert E. Baldwin and others, *Trade, Growth, and the Balance of Payments, Essays in Honor of Gottfried Haberler* (Rand McNally, 1965), pp. 3–34.

adequate capital market would provide funds for the lean years (months) until new industry matured. Indeed, only repayment of principal and interest without tariff protection would vindicate new industry, since early losses must be held to social account. Learning has its social opportunity costs.

If there are spinoffs from establishing a new enterprise such that the technology is more easily copied by other firms and/or more generalized labor-force training takes place, then publicly subsidized pilot projects or vocational training (quite different from tariff protection) would suffice. In order to qualify for subsidy, the purely external learning effects in the infant industry must be demonstrably greater than they are in those industries that are taxed to raise the subsidy. Even with this optimal public policy, however, "infant" entrepreneurs will still need a functioning capital market for intertemporal allocation in the learning phase and in the succeeding growth phases of the new industry.

2. *Import Licenses and Financial Leverage.* Licensing imports of capital goods and intermediate inputs is now common practice in underdeveloped economies. Although the reasons for initiating licensing are many and varied, they confer significant operating advantages on particular entrepreneurs, in contrast to tariff protection, which is nonspecific in this respect. The privilege of importing at a low price is another form of subsidy, which, like tariff protection, also increases the wealth or cash flow of producers.

But unlike general tariff protection, the exclusiveness of a license to import key materials may enable its holder to obtain external financing more easily. It is dramatically visible evidence to potential lenders of the future profitability of this *particular* enterprise. Public authorities consciously use licenses to manipulate the leverage of specific firms. Indeed, import licenses are frequently part of a package that includes short-term domestic bank finance (perhaps also subsidized) and foreign supplier credits. Thus the restraint on leverage is somewhat relaxed by the licensing mechanism.

Of course, detailed import licensing brings incredible bureaucratic inefficiencies,[2] but the underlying financial problem is not

2. See Ian Little, Tibor Scitovsky, and Maurice Scott, *Industry and Trade in Some Developing Countries: A Comparative Study* (London: Oxford University Press for Organisation for Economic Co-operation and Development, 1970).

trivial. In a fragmented economy, tariff protection by itself in a given industry may well encourage a large number of domestic entrepreneurs, each operating on a very small scale because of his limited initial endowment. Uncertainty as to which firm will prevail, combined with the general myopia of the capital market, may continue to limit severely the leverage available to any one entrepreneur. The inefficiencies of this form of "monopolistic competition" in protected markets that are already small have been widely noted.[3] It arises naturally out of our Fisherian model of a fragmented capital market that was shown in Figure 2-1.

Forced consolidation may be brought about by concentrating import licenses for crucial inputs in relatively few hands so as to reduce the fragmentation. Of course, the offsetting social cost is the creation of monopoly power. Cartel-like industrial structures manipulated by the licensing authorities are common in underdeveloped countries. The Colombian experience is not atypical, as Pakistan and India attest. The worst of both worlds occurs when limited licenses are distributed widely to avoid monopoly, so that fragmentation is maintained even as competition is dampened.

*3. Corruption and Monopoly Privilege.* Conferring monopoly privilege under implicit or explicit state sanction goes far beyond the granting of import licenses. Cheap bank credit and tax concessions for "essential" industries or firms are commonplace, as is privileged access to domestic fuel supplies and the outputs of other state-owned industries.[4] The resulting web of privilege, indistinguishable from corruption, and monopoly pricing with its well known drawbacks soon become counter-productive.

3. See Richard R. Nelson, T. Paul Schultz, and Robert L. Slighton, *Structural Change in a Developing Economy: Colombia's Problems and Prospects* (Princeton University Press, 1971).

4. In advanced economies, there is some history of the use of monopoly concessions to raise capital: the Hudson's Bay Company in North America in the seventeenth century and, more recently, the Communications Satellite Corporation in the United States are examples. On the other hand, Andrew Jackson vetoed the charter of the Bank of the United States because he felt it put too much capital at the disposal of a small group of men—even though he recognized the Bank's importance for achieving aggregate financial stability. A case can be made for carefully identifying "natural monopolies" in this way. There is no presumption, however, that the technique of monopoly charters for raising capital should be extended to activities other than natural monopolies in rich or poor countries.

Still, without a functioning capital market there is substantial pressure to extend state privileges so that the recipient can obtain financing to get a new fertilizer plant built or to exploit a new mineral deposit or perform some other essential function. This favoritism toward an "in" group of entrepreneurs cannot be explained away as pure corruption. Disequilibrium commodity prices arising from other interventions also add to the likelihood of corruption. But it would be a mistake to conclude that corruption is endemic in the underdeveloped environment. In an appropriately liberalized economy, one would expect it to be no more common than elsewhere.

*4. Cheapening of Capital Goods.* Moving away from purely microeconomic arguments in favor of helping specific firms or industries, restrictions on foreign trade tilt the whole structure of relative prices, reducing them in certain broad classes of commodities as it raises them in others. The costs in domestic currency of imported machinery and industrial inputs, whether or not they are licensed, are reduced substantially, as is shown in Chapter 10. If planners feel that overall capital accumulation is inadequate, why not reduce the relative prices of the essential ingredients of capital formation? The idea is easy to promote if the need for financial leverage within the enterprise buying these cheapened intermediate products is thereby reduced. It seems like an inexpensive technique for deploying the economy's surplus toward capital accumulation without using a capital market.

This reasoning implies acceptance of the doctrine of uniformly productive capital and ignores the need for rationalized intertemporal and inter-entrepreneur allocations. Of course, it encourages the overuse of imported capital goods. Ubiquitous excess capacity in plant and equipment and the adoption of overly mechanized "modern" production techniques with imported components can be explained in part by official policy that cheapens their relative costs. Yet it remains a plausible tenet of the authorities who govern foreign trade policy that imports of "essential" goods should be encouraged while "inessential" ones are kept out if industrialization is to be promoted.

*5. Agriculture's Terms of Trade.* The same manipulation of commodity prices designed to protect the nascent industrialist places a heavy burden on agriculture, indirectly through tariff and other industrial protection and directly through devices for reducing agricultural prices. For example, beef exports have been curtailed at various times in Uruguay, Argentina, and Brazil in order to keep urban food prices low; and raw jute and cotton exports have been curbed in Pakistan to provide cheap inputs for manufacturing activities. Doubling the price of manufactured goods in terms of agricultural produce through the combined effect of tariffs and export curbs was not uncommon in the postwar period.[5] It is not surprising that such policies have devastated rural incomes in many countries.

Yet this impoverishment of agriculture has been condoned by governments that are convinced that the rural economic "surplus" —whether in the form of redundant labor or of inferior savings opportunities—somehow had to be transferred to the industrial sector, where investment opportunities seemed more favorable. Financial mechanisms for inducing agricultural savers to part with their surplus voluntarily, at the posited high rates of return to be earned in industry, were implicitly assumed to be nonoperative. Thus the transfer took place through the expropriation of agriculture to provide an unrequited subsidy to industry.

In the mid-1960s, a reaction against the inequities and inefficiencies of the policy followed in the immediate postwar period partly restored agriculture's terms of trade in some countries.[6] The green revolution made agricultural investments look more attractive to policymakers. Nevertheless, fragmentation of capital markets within each sector, as well as their mutual isolation, leave the underlying problem unsolved.

For example, authorities are now tempted to raise the short-run price of particular crops that seem like good candidates for new

5. For the case of Pakistan, see Stephen R. Lewis, Jr., *Pakistan: Industrialization and Trade Policies* (London: Oxford University Press for OECD, 1970), pp. 22, 64, 86.

6. See, for example, Joel Bergsman, *Brazil: Industrialization and Trade Policies* (London: Oxford University Press for OECD, 1970); Carlos F. Díaz-Alejandro, "An Interpretation of Argentine Economic Growth Since 1930," Pt. 1, *Journal of Development Studies*, Vol. 3 (October 1966), pp. 14–41, and Pt. 2 in Vol. 3 (January 1967), pp. 155–77; and Stephen R. Lewis, Jr., "Effects of Trade Policy on Domestic Relative Prices: Pakistan, 1951–64," *American Economic Review*, Vol. 58 (March 1968), pp. 60–78.

agricultural techniques. A farm price support program provides both security for outside financing and increased cash flow; both encourage investment in new equipment or new seeds, pesticides, and so on, for the favored crops. Indeed, this policy had been advocated by some economists for modernizing U.S. agriculture in the 1940s.[7] One can expect officially induced oscillations in agriculture's terms of trade with the rest of the economy to continue until the capital constraint is relaxed.

6. *Land Reform.* The impoverishment of agriculture generates popular ferment to share the limited wealth more widely. Land is a very important form of endowment, which is tangible and highly visible; at the same time, limited leverage increases the importance of initial endowments in defining production opportunities. It is not surprising that land redistribution should be the principal policy followed in efforts to equalize current and future incomes in agrarian economies. Egalitarianism per se can hardly be faulted when differences in landholding are extreme and when nonagricultural production opportunities are severely limited for those without the necessary capital.

Yet there is another closely related aspect of land reform which, for many countries, is no less important than the egalitarian motive. Small as average landholdings may be, further fragmentation into tiny parcels is by no means uncommon. Minhas calculates that the mean landholding of individual farm families (excluding landless laborers) in India is only about 5.0 acres—which itself severely limits the income gains to the poor to be had from the redistribution of land.[8] Furthermore, these small holdings are divided, on an average, into about six noncontiguous parcels of less than one acre each. (Similar parcelization, albeit in somewhat larger pieces, is common in rural France.) Land fragmentation in India has increased visibly over the past ten years.

In order to use irrigation facilities, new technologies, and rural labor properly, Minhas advocates a massive consolidation program for existing holdings. Essentially, this would amount to publicly

7. D. Gale Johnson, *Forward Prices for Agriculture* (University of Chicago Press, 1947).

8. B. S. Minhas, "Rural Poverty, Land Redistribution and Development Strategy: Facts and Policy" (International Bank for Reconstruction and Development, Economic Development Institute, September 1970; processed).

enforced multilateral land barter, with improvements and other gradations in quality being weighted by official rules of thumb in determining each farmer's just share. Even though it runs the risk of not taking individual situations properly into account, the case for such a rationalization of Indian agriculture seems strong.

Why don't individuals bring about their own consolidation and comprehensive land development? Putting aside important questions of externalities and ignorance of payoffs, which Minhas emphasizes, if each farmer had free access to external finance, he could initiate bilateral action to buy contiguous pieces of land from a neighbor without waiting for government action. *A* could purchase parcels from *B*, who in turn bought from *C*, who eventually purchased from *A*, and so on. Land consolidation could accompany or be motivated by irrigation or green revolution prospects. However, the requisite external finance or internal liquidity is unlikely to be available.

But if post-reform landholdings are not to revert to fragments through the same inheritance and forced-sale patterns that were responsible for the problem in the first place, an improved capital market may still be considered necessary. Certainly if proper inducements to invest and improve the land are maintained, more than one arbitrary realignment of landholding must be avoided. At the same time, the freedom to sell land at an appropriately capitalized value, or to pledge land as collateral for loans, is important for encouraging agricultural improvements. Thus prohibitions on the resale of land are to be avoided—however much one wants to prevent new fragmentation or more inequality after the reform.

Such sanctions against resale damaged the efficiency of the Mexican land reform of the 1920s. The productivity of ejidos (land parcels distributed in the reform) is far below that of commercial farms (land unaffected by the reform) because there had been fewer improvements and because large segments of the rural labor force felt constrained to remain on the ejidos in suboptimal employment. Ejido holders lost their property rights upon leaving. Moreover, without the possibility of resale, land could not be used as collateral to obtain external financing. As a result, there was continuing discontent with the banks in rural areas. In a more liberalized environment where the capital market functioned efficiently, income redistribution (not confined to land reform) could equalize future incomes and opportunities without such losses of efficiency.

7. *Foreign Direct Investment and Commercial Credits: The Siren's Call.* In no aspect of economic policy do authorities in poor countries display more ambivalence than in that concerning the absorption of foreign capital. This love-hate relationship has economic roots that are deeper than the passing political events that trigger policy reversals. Direct investment from abroad by international corporations may be welcomed with tax concessions over some time intervals, only to be followed by periods of xenophobia, which include the threat of nationalization. In the mid-1950s, Brazil eliminated most of its severe restrictions on direct foreign investment and courted it actively, so that there were large inflows. A complete policy reversal in 1959 dried up the inflow; and then in 1964 the welcome mat was out again.

If the domestic capital market is moribund, then the use of foreign financial services becomes more attractive. Nevertheless, direct investment may be expensive because the risk foreigners see in operating in the domestic economy is greater than that seen by domestic nationals. More fundamentally, our fragmentation hypothesis suggests that domestic entrepreneurs have investment opportunities but lack financing from outside their own enterprise to exploit these opportunities. Relying on direct investment from abroad may break the external financial constraint at the cost of relinquishing investment opportunities to foreigners at bargain-basement prices. Domestic entrepreneurial development may thereby be retarded. Learning-by-doing becomes learning-by-watching. The government may respond with complex bureaucratic controls to ensure national participation in foreign enterprise, but these bring their own inefficiencies.

Chapter 12 analyzes the whole question of absorbing foreign capital efficiently—direct investment, supplier credits, and foreign aid. Here it suffices to note the pressure to rely excessively on foreign sources of finance if internal financial arteries are clogged. Correspondingly there is a danger of returning to the "colonial" economy, where expatriates operate with relatively freer access to an external capital market in such a way as to emasculate domestic entrepreneurial development.

## Self-Finance and the Distribution of Income

Can one generalize at all about this lengthy catalogue of public policies for circumventing the domestic capital market? The bias toward self-finance is one common thread. "Self-finance" is defined as the investment within a particular enterprise (or economic unit) of savings accumulated in that enterprise. Public interventions relieve the constraint on external finance by enriching the holder of a production opportunity, or by making that opportunity appear to be more profitable so that the immediate cash flow from it is increased. Raising output prices through tariffs or other subsidies has just this effect. Not infrequently, the recipient of the subsidy is a foreign firm.

Using prices to generate cash flows for investment distorts their allocative function in either public or private planning. Rationing and black markets abound, and prices no longer indicate true social cost. However, behind it lies a view of the savings–investment process that appears to be fundamentally incorrect. It has been implicitly assumed that the quality of investment and the flow of new saving are both independent of the reward structure.

Firms in a particular industry that the government wants to encourage by raising its relative price or by granting it import licenses have their incomes increased regardless of how efficiently they operate. They receive a subsidy, only a part of which may be invested, and the social distribution of income is tilted in their favor. In practice, a part of the subsidy is appropriated by industrialists and another part by urban labor groups, which can and do set very high wages for their industry—perhaps several times the wage level in the country as a whole. Basically there is no system of social accountability for the use of this subsidy, and its incidence may be different from that intended. Thus the general efficiency of resource use is low and shows surprisingly little tendency to improve.[9]

Obversely, changing the commodity terms of trade in favor of manufactured goods extracts forced saving elsewhere—particularly in rural areas—without compensation. It is argued, in defense of

9. Henry J. Bruton, "Productivity Growth in Latin America," *American Economic Review,* Vol. 57 (December 1967), pp. 1099–1116.

that policy, that those in the industrial-urban sector may save more out of given incomes than do rural people, so that the transfer increases total saving; but there is no statistical evidence of this, and it is not plausible a priori. Clearly, the link between this form of saving and the reward for saving is broken. It is hardly surprising that voluntary domestic saving is limited.

From another point of view, self-finance tilts the distribution of income toward the rich in urban areas, who already have some resources. Thus economic stratification is tightened, while highly productive investment opportunities are passed up.

## *Unemployment and Factor Proportions:*
## *Rates of Interest Again*

Unemployment has replaced famine as the number one political and economic problem in less developed countries. Heavily subsidized industrialization has done little to relieve unemployment, and it is now a general phenomenon in both rural and urban sectors.[10] Briefly, what is the relationship between our hypothesized capital constraint and factor proportions—the ratios in which labor, land, and capital are used in production processes?

The capital constraint has affected factor proportions: (1) through public interventions to circumvent it, and (2) more directly by limiting the external investment opportunities that savers and the holders of capital have. The first is directly evident from our catalogue of public interventions. For example, inexpensive and relatively easily financed imports of intermediate products lead to over-mechanization in the heavily protected industrial enclaves. But even without such interventions, self-finance can induce forms of overinvestment.

Consider the position of the individual Pakistani or Indian farmer who successfully invests in new seeds and fertilizers (perhaps with some aid from external finance) so that his internal cash flow is greatly increased. (Incidentally, the cultivation required by these new seed-fertilizer technologies is highly labor intensive.) After paying his debts, he wants to save something from his new

10. David Turnham, assisted by Ingelies Jaeger, *The Employment Problem in Less Developed Countries: a Review of Evidence* (Paris: Development Centre of the Organisation for Economic Co-operation and Development, 1971), pp. 9–11.

surplus, but high-yielding assets from outside his own enterprise are not available to him. Further internal investment then is the only avenue open. Replacing his bullocks and hired labor with a new tractor may be the next project on his preference ordering.

There is a strong likelihood that the seed-fertilizer revolution will give an impetus to premature tractor mechanization. The rapid initial increase in cash income, especially in Pakistan, India, and other countries where rapid import substitution is taking place, increases the ability and the incentive to invest in such equipment. In economies in which little structural transformation has occurred and the absolute size of the farm labor force is increasing rapidly, investment in tractor mechanization is likely to be uneconomic from society's point of view even though it is profitable to the large farm operators. Their saving in labor costs as determined by market wage rates is likely to be considerably higher than the marginal productivity of the labor that is displaced. The social costs of exacerbating problems of underemployment and unemployment do not enter into their assessment of costs and returns.[11]

The problem is not confined to agriculture. Excess capacity in plant and equipment in urban areas may, to some degree, be a manifestation of the same phenomenon. Internal cash flow is re-invested in low-priority uses within the generating firm. Furthermore, if inflation drives real rates of return on all financial assets to negative values, it is not difficult to imagine that some internal investments within "surplus" industrial enterprise also would generate negative real rates of return.

In Chapter 2, a Fisherian model was developed that linked external financing and high rates of interest on financial assets with the efficient diffusion of modern technology. "Efficiency" in this context meant that factor scarcity was accurately taken into account as new techniques were adopted through increased internal investment. Paradoxically, the same high rates of interest on financial assets may be necessary to prevent *premature modernization* or mechanization through increased internal investment within an individual enterprise! The well off Pakistani farmer might open a new savings account rather than buy a new tractor. The industrialist might reduce his investment in his own plant capacity or inventories used as an inflation hedge, in order to acquire commercial

11. Bruce F. Johnston and John Cownie, "The Seed-Fertilizer Revolution and Labor Force Absorption," *American Economic Review*, Vol. 59 (September 1969), p. 574.

claims on other firms at higher real rates of return. Unfortunately these options are seldom open in underdeveloped countries.

Unlike the neoclassical view, factor proportions are not governed by a single rate of interest and a single real wage rate. Rather, fragmentation contributes significantly to underemployment in some areas and overinvestment in others.

## The Tax-Subsidy Solution and the Theory of the Second-Best

Even without a unified view of the causes of state intervention, foreign trade theorists have long recognized the inefficiency of distorting commodity prices to achieve policy goals. In particular, a tariff or other trade restriction makes the domestic price structure diverge from the international one by raising the internal price of the protected commodity. If the aim is simply to stimulate production in a particular industry, the higher internal prices cause an unnecessary loss of efficiency by unduly restricting the consumption of its output. Hence, the well known proposition that a direct production subsidy, leaving price unchanged, is the "best" technique[12] for stimulating production to some predetermined level. The tariff is a second-best strategy and could diminish welfare even if there were some economically legitimate reason for stimulating production in one industry at the expense of others.

This traditional wisdom is important, and eliminating unnecessary price distortions is a key element in the liberalization process. There are, however, some important reservations. Since a fragmented economy faces severe fiscal constraints, financing a production subsidy by raising taxes generates its own distortions. A tariff on competing imports at least has the advantage of being fiscally sound in the sense that consumers of the output of the protected industry are effectively taxed to subsidize producers.

More fundamentally, the production subsidy does not recognize the nature of the capital constraint. First, the authorities must correctly identify an industry that is technologically backward or even

12. The word "best" is used here in the economist's sense to describe a technique or a policy that achieves some preassigned goal with the least social cost to consumers and to other producers.

nonexistent, but whose potential future productivity is high and to which it is to the comparative advantage of the economy to devote resources. Since production opportunities are widely scattered among individual firm–households, the authorities lack any reliable budgetary procedure for identifying future star performers and allocating production subsidies to them. Second, the production subsidy itself (like a tariff) retains the bias toward self-finance in the protected industry and does not recognize the fundamental role of an external financial structure in facilitating efficient decision making over time.

But if the distortion is in the factor markets—particularly that for capital—can it not be eliminated by subsidizing one or another of the primary factors of production? An extensive literature on international trade theory suggests that there is such a policy.[13] If one posits a distortion that *uniformly* raises the cost of capital in one identifiable sector of the economy, a case could be made for subsidizing the use of capital there, provided that the distortion itself is not thereby aggravated. Under these circumstances, the literature demonstrates that such a factor subsidy is a first-best policy, while a pure output subsidy would be only second-best, and a tariff would be third-best.

However, our fragmentation hypothesis indicates just how deceptive such a "standard" policy recommendation might be. Consider the situation in Pakistani and Indian agriculture. A uniform subsidy for all new capital investments, even if it were administratively feasible, might accelerate mechanization on some farms in the face of heavy rural unemployment, even as it hastened the adoption of new seeds and fertilizers on others. A selective subsidy confined to seeds and fertilizers would increase the internal cash flow of those farmers who did adopt the new methods; and this in time could also lead to undue mechanization. Tax-subsidies, tailored to a degree of fineness beyond the knowledge and administrative capacity of the government, cannot substitute for a financial system where borrowing and lending are undertaken freely at high rates

13. The most recent version of this theory is well summarized by Jagdish N. Bhagwati in "The Generalized Theory of Distortions and Welfare" in *Trade, Balance of Payments and Growth*, Papers in International Economics in Honor of Charles P. Kindleberger (American Elsevier, 1971), pp. 69–90; but the problem goes back a long way. See, for example, Mihail Manolescu, *The Theory of Protection and International Trade* (London: P. S. King, 1931).

of interest. Contrary to prevailing theory, a first-best fiscal solution cannot be found for what is essentially a financial problem.

Recommendations for subsidizing the use of labor in modern industry are more common than those for subsidizing capital in agriculture. Manolescu argued that it should be done indirectly through a tariff, and more recently an otherwise cautious study by the Organisation for Economic Co-operation and Development (OECD) suggested that "the main encouragement to manufacturing, via the price mechanism, would then be given by subsidizing unskilled labour."[14] But again, the degree of fragmentation and the magnitude of the labor problem make such policies almost impossible to implement and certainly unwise.

Consider a typical textile manufacturing industry where there is a spectrum ranging from home handicraft work, using very simple equipment, to large "organized" firms with fairly modern plant and machinery, which may or may not be fully utilized. The usual pattern is for the wage rate in the modern sector to be much higher—especially if the industry has grown up behind a tariff wall. What criterion for the labor subsidy should the government use? The Colombian, Venezuelan, and Puerto Rican experiences suggest that organized labor in the modern sector is quite adept at appropriating any form of subsidy through wage increases so that additional labor absorption is blocked. At the same time, one would feel chary about subsidizing a highly mechanized producer to employ more labor if the subsidy would increase his internal cash flow. Should a small-scale, labor-using handicraft industry not be subsidized? Again, the appropriate rate of technological diffusion and the efficient absorption of labor are basically financial rather than fiscal problems.[15]

What role then remains for fiscal policy in using differentiated taxes and subsidies directed toward particular industries? Apart from macroeconomic stabilization policies, the tax machinery of

14. Little and others, *Industry and Trade,* p. 331.

15. The employment problem is sufficiently acute in LDCs that the Organisation for Economic Co-operation and Development commissioned a study on using fiscal policy to alleviate unemployment (*Fiscal Policy and the Employment Problem in Less Developed Countries,* by Alan Peacock and G. K. Shaw [OECD, 1971]). Peacock and Shaw outlined a detailed set of criteria for subsidizing labor-intensive activities in order to increase employment, even if it meant accepting a reduction in real output in economies already very poor.

the government can be fully employed financing "public" goods (according to accepted canons of public finance), redistributing income, and mobilizing an economic surplus of revenues over current expenditure for capital formation. Some of the capital formation would be internalized within the public sector, but some—as was the case in Japan—could actually be passed through an efficient financial mechanism to capital accumulation elsewhere in the domestic economy in nonauthoritarian regimes. This would leave little or no room for a web of industrial subsidies and tax rebates, such as now exists in many poor countries, to substitute for a viable financial mechanism in allocating private and public capital. Techniques for achieving fiscal neutrality are discussed in Chapter 10 as part of the general liberalization process.

# 4

## Money and the Price Level

IF FISCAL AND OTHER substitutes for financial processes have
been found wanting both in theory and in practice, how can the
government nurture domestic capital markets in fragmented economies? In this and in immediately following chapters, the pecu-
liarly important role of the domestic monetary system in improving the quality and quantity of capital formation is analyzed.
(Consideration of foreign sources of finance will be deferred, and
the discussion will proceed as if the economy were completely dependent on the domestic capital market.)

First, consider the nature of the financial structure now found
in poor countries outside of the communist bloc. Raymond Goldsmith[1] has shown that: (1) individual economic units issue relatively few primary securities as a proportion of saving—thus indicating the greater reliance placed on self-finance by firms within
the developing countries in comparison with firms in wealthy
countries; (2) most of this limited flow of primary securities is acquired by financial institutions rather than being placed directly
with final savers; and (3) the liabilities of the monetary system—
the central bank plus deposit banks—account for about two-thirds
of all claims on intermediary financial institutions that are held by

1. *Financial Structure and Development* (Yale University Press, 1969), Chaps. 1
and 9, and "The Development of Financial Institutions During the Post-War Period,"
in *Banca Nazionale del Lavoro Quarterly Review*, No. 97 (Rome: June 1971), pp.
129–92.

the public. Apparently, there are few "organized" markets for such primary securities as bonds, mortgages, or common stock, since they require economies of scale that are generally not present in the less developed countries.[2] In short, there is little direct contact between the primary borrower and the ultimate lender. Rather, indirect financing or intermediation through the monetary mechanism is the main artery of the "modern" financial sector, which itself may be quite limited. In analyzing poor countries, therefore, it is sometimes quite reasonable to develop theoretical models where money, $M$, which is broadly defined to include interest- and noninterest-bearing deposits of the banking system, as well as currency, is the only financial asset available to wealth holders. In mature economies, on the other hand, there is a much wider spectrum of available financial assets, some of which may be fairly close substitutes for money.

Why should the monetary system dominate the limited financial structure of less developed countries, even when it has been heavily taxed by inflation or other official policies? Uncertainty about the future exists in all economies, but this uncertainty is particularly acute in poor countries, as was pointed out in Chapter 2. Since money is legally designated as the medium of exchange, it is uniquely risk- and default-free for short-term transactions. The cost of buying and selling money for real goods is low, both for the owner of cash balances and for the banking system, which supplies checking services, mints coins, and prints notes. Since creditors know little or nothing about the repayment capability of potential debtors in underdeveloped countries, financial instruments other than money cannot easily be marketed. Hence, money's role as a means of payment, and its sanction by the state, greatly enhance its value as an instrument of private capital accumulation—the exact sense to be outlined below.

Money's usefulness as a financial instrument, however, depends on the willingness of our firm–households (whose characteristics were defined in Chapter 2) to hold it. Over finite time intervals,

---

2. On the other hand, traditional curb markets are sometimes important, deserve careful study, and deserve something more than the official hostility to which they have often been subject, as is illustrated in Chapter 7. The "curb" or traditional capital market is associated with small-scale rural and urban moneylending or pawnbroking—sometimes supplemented by rural cooperatives.

no real or financial asset is riskless. Money's attractiveness depends on some combination of the percentage rate[3] of inflation, $\dot{P}$ ($P$ being a comprehensive price index of goods in terms of money), the nominal interest rate on deposits, $d$, and the "convenience" of holding money—particularly in demand deposits and currency. In practice, $\dot{P}$ is neither stable nor perfectly predictable in poor countries. Initially, "long-run" models of money holding and capital accumulation are developed here, where individuals anticipate movements in the price level. This decision horizon need not be long in a purely temporal sense because expected future rates of inflation may change quickly. Individuals can rapidly adapt their holdings of real money balances, $M/P$, to the real return on holding money that they anticipate.

As a convenient short-hand term, the real return on holding money will be denoted here by $d - \dot{P}*$, where $\dot{P}*$ is the expected future rate of inflation. The symbol $d$ is to be interpreted as a weighted average of nominal interest rates on all classes of deposits, including currency. Once *ex ante* expectations as to this real return on holding money are established, a stable demand for real cash balances can be posited for any given level of income.

The instruments of monetary policy open to the authorities are the nominal interest rate on deposits, $d$, and the rate of expansion in *nominal* cash balances, $\dot{M}$. How then are $\dot{P}$ and $\dot{P}*$ determined?

Interaction between the demand for and supply of money is the prime mover of the price level in the approach to be followed here; and it is also the working assumption used by modern monetary "growth theorists." If the supply of nominal money rises faster than the demand for real balances, price inflation ensues.[4] This demand for real balances will be positively linked to the rate of growth in real output, as well as being strongly influenced by the real return on holding money, and can rise more than in proportion to output in times of rapid economic transformation. Nevertheless, $\dot{M}$ eventually determines the actual and ultimately the ex-

3. The convention is followed here of using a superscript, · , to represent proportional rather than absolute changes through time in the designated variable. That is,

$$\dot{P} = (dP/dt)/P.$$

4. In contrast, Keynesian theory emphasizes divergences between *ex ante* flows of investment and savings in order to establish an "inflationary gap," which can move the price level under conditions of full employment.

pected rate of change in the price level. The authorities, therefore, can indirectly set the real return on money, $d - \dot{P}*$, at whatever level they believe to be socially desirable.

Of course, causality runs both ways. The rate of price inflation, as determined by $\dot{M}$, can affect the rate of growth of real output both in the short and in the long run. This reverse causality operates through the impact of monetary policy on the accumulation of physical capital. That is, monetary policy strongly affects private propensities to save and invest in the underdeveloped economy. Later chapters will show how this impact differs from that suggested by both neoclassical and Keynesian monetary theory. These relationships are quite intricate, however; and for now, we simply assume that the monetary authority knows how to manipulate $\dot{M}$ to achieve a desired $\dot{P}$ by taking into account any changes in real output that the authority's own actions might induce.

This real return on holding money can be highly negative and unstable in inflationary regimes, such as those found in many Latin American countries; or it can be substantially greater than zero in those few countries, such as Korea and Taiwan, that have recently chosen to keep $d$ high and $\dot{P}$ relatively small. Nevertheless, the public's demand for *real* money still determines the volume of $M/P$ outstanding at whatever average real rate of return on money, and variance in that rate, the government sees fit to select. Chapter 8 presents evidence that firms and households in poor countries are quite sensitive to $d - \dot{P}*$ in determining their preferred ratio of money holdings to income.

For the underdeveloped economy, it will be demonstrated that the demand for real cash balances and the demand for physical capital are highly *complementary* in private asset portfolios, in contrast to prevailing theory, where a substitution relationship is dominant. That is, conditions that make $M/P$ attractive to hold enhance rather than inhibit private incentives to accumulate physical capital. In turn, large real money holdings are normally the result of the monetary system's maintaining a high and stable real return to the holders of money. This complementarity hypothesis leads to policy conclusions about inflationary finance, and about deposit rates of interest for accelerating development, that are quite different from the corpus of accepted monetary theory. Both neoclassical and Keynesian theories were designed for mature economies with functioning capital markets and may be quite harmful if uncritically applied to the fragmented economic environment described in Chapter 2.

It is convenient, therefore, to review in Chapter 5 some standard propositions inherent in monetary growth theory regarding the long-run determinants of investment and saving. Readers who are not directly interested in current monetary controversy, or those not burdened by the dead weight of past ideas, may wish to pass over lightly the critique immediately following. In any event, references back to specific portions of the neoclassical argument will be made in the course of developing an alternative model of money and capital accumulation in Chapter 6 and succeeding chapters.

# 5

# A Critique of Prevailing
# Monetary Theory

THIS CHAPTER IS CONCERNED with that portion of prevailing theory that takes a fairly long view of monetary and fiscal policy in determining the rate of capital accumulation and growth in real output, and that relates the formation of prices and price expectations to the issue of nominal money, as was described in Chapter 4. The Keynesian model, which has a more purely short-run orientation toward income and employment and assumes relatively fixed prices, is not analyzed until later—and then not in any detail. Instead, the vast literature on what is now known as neoclassical growth theory is the main object of this critique.[1] This is not to imply, however, that the Keynesian model is any more relevant than its "monetarist" or neoclassical counterpart when it is applied to the peculiar problems of the less developed countries.

The basic neoclassical assumptions of particular significance for our purposes are:

1. Major representative authors are Milton Friedman (*The Optimum Quantity of Money and Other Essays* [Aldine, 1969]); Harry G. Johnson ("Money in a Neo-Classical One-Sector Growth Model," in *Essays in Monetary Economics* [Harvard University Press, 1967]); David Levhari and Don Patinkin ("The Role of Money in a Simple Growth Model," *American Economic Review*, Vol. 58 [September 1968], pp. 713–53); Robert Mundell (*Monetary Theory: Inflation, Interest and Growth in the World Economy* [Goodyear, 1971]).

1. Capital markets operate perfectly and costlessly to equate returns on all real and financial assets (other than money) with a single real rate of interest—the nominal rate that reflects expected inflation accurately. Indeed, in some models, all nonmonetary assets are perfect substitutes intramarginally in the portfolios of savers. The processes of saving and investing can be quite specialized between distinct groups of households and firms.

2. Inputs (including capital) and outputs are perfectly divisible, with constant returns to scale in the prototype enterprise. Production within an individual firm can always be considered a miniature replica of the aggregate production function, with all firms having access to the same technology and to the same prices in commodity and factor markets.

3. There is an important transactions demand for money in avoiding the need for the well known "double coincidence of wants." Money, however, plays no direct role in capital accumulation per se because assumption 1, above, implies a perfect market in physical capital and interest-bearing claims on it.

4. Real money balances are virtually socially costless to produce for satisfying this transactions motive. The costs of minting coins and clearing checks are trivial relative to the benefits that money confers. Hence, money can be thought of as the "outside" fiat type being issued by the government for current services, and there is no meaningful distinction between currency and deposits.

These four assumptions, whether they are explicit or implicit, simplify what is now known as monetary growth theory. Indeed simplification is necessary in any general equilibrium model. Such authors as Milton Friedman, Harry Johnson, David Levhari and Don Patinkin, and Robert Mundell[2] all use these assumptions to generate similar conclusions about the demand for money, although their approaches differ in detail and in emphasis. For example, there is a choice of convenience between treating real money balances, $M/P$, as a producer's or as a consumer's good in order to generate a demand for it. In either case, money is treated as a form of wealth that competes with other assets in the portfolios of consumers and producers.

2. Cited in note 1, above.

## Substitution between Money and Physical Capital

The term "substitution effect" is used to indicate the possibility that large real cash balances will inhibit the accumulation of physical capital in the private sector. It is quite easy to see how this substitution effect in private demands to hold money or capital can be derived from the premises of traditional theory.

Consider the standard algebraic format of the money-demand function arising out of the four assumptions listed above. Let $Y$ denote aggregate real income, and let $r$ denote "the" real rate of return on both physical capital and all nonmonetary financial assets. Hence $r$ less the real return on money, $d - \dot{P}^*$, is the opportunity cost to wealth holders of holding money. More formally, a function describing the *equilibrium* demand for money, in the sense of a target that is independent of what current cash balance holdings happen to be, can be written:

$$(5\text{-}1) \qquad (M/P)^D = H(Y, r, d - \dot{P}^*),$$

where $\partial H / \partial Y > 0$, $\partial H / \partial r < 0$, and $\partial H / \partial (d - \dot{P}^*) > 0$.

It should be remembered that the rate of price inflation is automatically built into "the" nominal yield on assets other than money. The nominal rate of return on money itself, however, does not adjust automatically to the expected rate of inflation because it is administratively difficult to pay interest on currency and demand deposits. Hence for any given nominal interest rate $d$ (possibly zero) that is paid on deposits, inflation will reduce the real return on money. Thus $r$ and $d - \dot{P}^*$ are the comparable rates of return on the two assets available to potential wealth holders at a given income level, as shown by the function $H$ in equation 5-1.

Within this simplified version of the neoclassical model, $\partial H / \partial r < 0$. What is the intuitive economic rationale for this negative impact of an increase in $r$ on the demand for money? Money is held because of its usefulness as a medium of exchange, whereas capital (or claims on capital) is held for its own *separable* rate of return. With a rise in $r$, individual assetholders switch, at the margin, from money to more lucrative physical capital. In doing so, they give up some of the transactions advantages of using money. Symmetrically, an increase in the real return on holding money, for a given $Y$ and $r$, reduces the demand for physical capital in the portfolios of private savers. This is the *substitution effect* between money and real capital, which dominates neoclassical monetary theory.

Moving away from a purely stationary analysis of an individual household or firm choosing *ex ante* between these two assets, consider now the substitution effect between money and aggregate investment for an economy moving on a balanced growth path. In the technical note to this chapter, the monetary growth model of Levhari and Patinkin[3]—which I believe accurately describes the recent view of Milton Friedman, Harry G. Johnson, James Tobin, and others[4]—is used to derive the neoclassical investment function that holds in equilibrium growth:

$$(5\text{-}2) \qquad I = dK/dt = sY + (s - 1)(\dot{M} - \dot{P})M/P,$$
$$\text{and } (s - 1)(\dot{M} - \dot{P}) < 0,$$

where $Y$ is the current output of goods and services (aggregate income, not including the change in the value of real cash balances), $s$ is the marginal propensity to save (abstinence from current consumption), $I$ is the aggregate annual flow of investment in physical capital, $K$ is the stock of physical capital, and $t$ is an index of time.

A key characteristic of this investment function is that an increase in demand for the real stock of money *reduces* investment, as is reflected by the negative[5] coefficient of $M/P$ in equation 5-2. The intuitive rationale for this algebraic result is analogous to that used in the stationary model of asset choice. With a given propensity to save, $s$, actual saving will be directed either toward real money balances or toward physical capital. Consequently, if the real return on money were to rise so as to make it more attractive to hold $M/P$ at any given level of income, investment in physical capital would decline.

Might not this portfolio-substitution effect be offset by a rise in

3. "Role of Money."

4. See note 1, above, and James Tobin, "Notes on Optimal Monetary Growth," *Journal of Political Economy*, Vol. 76 (July/August 1968), Pt. 2, pp. 833–59.

5. Because the marginal propensity to save is less than unity, $s - 1 < 0$; and $\dot{M} - \dot{P} > 0$ because the rate of issue of nominal money is always greater than the rate of increase in the price level in a growing economy.

the private propensity to save when the real return on holding money is raised? Authors writing in this neoclassical tradition usually take $s$ as given—partly for mathematical convenience and partly because it is hard to justify an upward shift in $s$ under assumptions 1 through 3, above. In saving over extended periods of time, individuals already have the option of holding nonmonetary financial claims or perfectly divisible physical assets reflecting the real return to capital as well as the rate of inflation. Since cash balances are not needed as a store of value in the context of the neoclassical model, the private propensity to save is often assumed to be invariant to the real return on holding money, and hence it is invariant to monetary policy generally.

While not according money any particular significance in the acquisition of physical capital per se, most authors have recognized that cash balances are a valuable *current* input into production processes as a medium of exchange. Levhari and Patinkin[6] were careful to include $M/P$ as an input like labor or capital in the aggregate production function, as is shown in the technical note to this chapter. It is possible, therefore, that the greater efficiency of larger cash balances in meeting transactions needs could increase output sufficiently to offset the declining share of output allocated to physical investment for sustaining economic growth. Although it is not likely, the equilibrium values of income and hence investments in equation 5-2 could conceivably rise with an increase in the real return on holding money. Neoclassical authors would consider that this positive effect of a higher real return on money would occur only in the extreme case where heavy inflation had severely impaired the usefulness of money as a medium of exchange.

Hence the portfolio substitution effect between $M/P$ and physical capital (or investment), at any given level of output, remains a crucial part of accepted monetary theory. *Within this neoclassical model, authorities who want to encourage private investment may well be chary of policies that raise $M/P$.*[7]

6. In "The Role of Money in a Simple Growth Model."

7. In Keynesian monetary theory, this substitution effect between money and real capital enters more strongly. "Hoarding" (presumably of cash balances) and liquidity traps abound to siphon off saving from productive physical investment—possibly leaving unemployed resources. Keynes himself toyed with ideas such as Gesell stamps. (John Maynard Keynes, *The General Theory of Employment, Interest and Money* [Harcourt, Brace, 1936], p. 357). The stamps were designed to reduce

## *The Golden Rule and the Full-Liquidity Rule*

How does the government manipulate the instruments of monetary and fiscal policy in order to maximize social welfare within the neoclassical framework? The money supply, $M$, or its rate of change, $\dot{M}$, can easily be controlled through the issue of nominal money as a transfer payment to the private sector, or in return for current services rendered by the private sector to the government. Alternatively, nominal money could be increased if the monetary system made loans to individuals or firms, although assumptions 1 and 4 offer assurance that the banking system has no particular comparative advantages as a financial intermediary. The nominal interest rate on certain classes of time and savings deposits can also be influenced by the authorities—although neoclassical theory provides no real rationale for distinguishing among various classes of "money."

What is the *modus operandi* of fiscal policy within this world of perfect capital markets? In contrast to Keynesian "fine tuning," fiscal policy is viewed primarily as a device for using public saving to control the rate of aggregate capital formation over the long run. To characterize this control problem as simply as possible, the following assumption on fiscal policy is added to the previous list.

5. Fiscal policy can be used costlessly to adjust the aggregate rate of capital formation by running a public-sector surplus (or deficit) to increase (or reduce) the stock of real capital. It makes no difference whether this is done by acquiring claims on (selling bonds to) the private sector or whether the stock of physical capital is directly bought and held by the government. Interest-bearing government bonds are a perfect substitute for real capital in the portfolios of private savers.

Thus armed with tractable instruments of monetary and fiscal policy, what targets should the government set for the rate of accumulation of physical capital and the level of outstanding real money balances? To some extent, the answers depend on whether

---

the real return on money and so reduce the willingness of individuals to hold real money balances.

the economy is on a balanced growth path, in a stationary state, or in some nonequilibrium position. However, there is an optimal monetary policy that does not require elaborate additional specifications about the state of the economy. This is the "full-liquidity rule" that has been extensively investigated by Milton Friedman.[8]

According to assumption 4, money—real or nominal—is costless to create and should not be economized on in any way. Nonetheless, money is still highly productive because of its role as a medium of exchange, and this productivity is related directly to the real size of cash balance holdings. Given the size of the capital stock, an expansion in $M/P$ increases aggregate output—albeit with diminishing marginal increments. (This process is described more formally in the technical note to this chapter.) Since $M/P$ is also socially costless to produce, it should be expanded in the portfolios of wealth holders until its marginal product falls to zero.

There is a snare, however, in securing the requisite expansion in $M/P$. Private wealth holders may have to be "bribed" to expand their holdings of real cash balances far enough to reduce the marginal product of money to zero. Money competes with physical capital in the portfolios of savers, as described by the neoclassical money-demand function $H$ in equation 5-1. Hence, at the margin, wealth holders will restrict $M/P$ to the point where the real return on money *plus* the "convenience" of holding money is equal to the return on capital. This condition of equilibrium in private portfolios can be described as follows:

(5-3)   $(d - \dot{P}^*)$ + marginal convenience yield of money $= r$.

In a condition of private portfolio balance, therefore, the marginal product of money normally is *positive* rather than zero. Essentially, private individuals react inappropriately to the social costlessness of creating money and feel constrained to keep their real cash balances too small because of the alternative possibility of holding physical capital. This private economizing wastes real resources of labor and capital in the search-and-barter process. Transactions costs throughout the economy remain unnecessarily high.

The government, however, need not suffer from social myopia

8. *The Optimum Quantity of Money.*

and can increase real cash balances by increasing the real return, $d - \dot{P}^*$. If $d$ is close to zero for the administrative reasons referred to above, then the government can set $\dot{M}$ so as to achieve steady *deflation*; that is, $\dot{P} < 0$. Moreover, it is not necessary to raise the real return on holding money above $r$, because massive portfolio changes from relatively illiquid nonmonetary wealth to highly liquid real money balances would occur once $d - \dot{P}^*$ approached $r$. Hence, the optimal strategy for securing full monetary liquidity can be described by the *full-liquidity rule*:

$$(5\text{-}4) \qquad\qquad d - \dot{P}^* = r.$$

Equation 5-4 implies that price deflation at rate $r$—the real return to capital—is socially optimal if no formal deposit rate of interest is paid on holdings of cash balances. Depending on its administrative feasibility, an alternative policy of having $d = r$, when the price level is stable, would be equally effective in securing full liquidity.

But what about real capital formation and growth? Might not a large expansion in $M/P$ reduce investment in physical capital as a proportion of income because of the substitution effect described above? Private saving could be siphoned off to maintain the large monetary hoards that the full-liquidity rule seems to portend. This unfortunate effect could well hold if private saving remained the only source of capital formation. Under assumption 5, however, the government is free to assign fiscal policy to increase public saving in order to compensate for the substitution effect in private portfolios.[9] Hence, the omniscient and omnipotent government can select whatever level of aggregate investment it deems to be socially optimal.

There are many possible paths for accumulation that the government might choose, all of which affect the intertemporal distribution of welfare. The one most commonly referred to in the literature is the "golden rule" of accumulation of physical capital,

9. As John Scadding has pointed out to the author, the fiscal authorities would not have this freedom if the private sector tended to consolidate government saving-investment decisions with its own behavior. Here the government may be powerless to influence aggregate saving because the private sector can always reduce its own saving in anticipating a fiscal surplus in the public sector. The criticism in this book of the neoclassical approach takes a different tack, as soon will become clear.

which calls for the maximization of per capita consumption along a balanced growth path. As is well known, this maximum is achieved when public plus private investment is adjusted so that the real rate of return on capital is equal to the rate of growth:

$$(5\text{-}5) \qquad\qquad r = \dot{Y}.$$

Thus optimization within the neoclassical model is neatly summarized by the golden and full-liquidity rules. Indeed, if golden-rule fiscal policy is carried out as defined in equation 5-5, and the nominal interest rate on deposits is zero, full-liquidity monetary policy consists simply of keeping the nominal stock of money fixed, so that prices decline at the same rate at which income grows. Combining the two optimizing rules contained in equations 5-4 and 5-5 yields:

$$(5\text{-}6) \qquad \dot{Y} = d - \dot{P}^* = r, \text{ with } \dot{M} = 0 \text{ if } d = 0.$$

The life of monetary authorities is indeed idyllic (and perhaps a bit dull) with only a little more effort required on the fiscal side to keep the rate of aggregate investment properly adjusted. The banking-monetary system has no particular role to play in the process of capital accumulation, even though bankers and their public relations officers may have persuaded people otherwise.

## Difficulties with the Neoclassical Approach and the Bias toward Inflation

Simplicity is a virtue, and it is a considerable intellectual achievement that a complex general-equilibrium model can be reduced to the easily comprehended golden and full-liquidity rules of optimizing behavior. Unfortunately the neoclassical model does not transfer well to poor, fragmented economies—even over a fairly "long" time horizon in which to select asset portfolios. It omits issues of particular importance to less developed countries, and contains unfortunate biases when it—or a slightly modified version of it—is used as a basis for policy.

The issues omitted are:

• the question of improving the quality of the capital stock by reducing dispersion in rates of return, that is, the whole problem of imperfect capital markets, which is so important;

• the optimal commitment of real resources to the monetary system; and

• the nature of fiscal constraints on government in adjusting the aggregate rate of capital accumulation.

These omissions then lead to biased conclusions regarding:

• the substitution effect between real money balances and real capital accumulation;

• the independence from monetary policy of the private rate of saving;

• the use of the inflation tax as an instrument to promote social saving; and

• the dominance of diminishing returns in capital accumulation.

Finally, there is the purely logical conundrum that:

• the basic assumptions of the model do not generate a determinate demand for money.

Biases of course can be judged only when an alternative "less biased" model is set up, as is done in Chapter 6. However, let us see how economic policy that is based on the neoclassical model is *prone to inflation* if it is applied to certain problems in poor countries. Suppose that the rate of capital accumulation is "obviously" too low, but the government does not have the capacity or will to use conventional taxing techniques to increase the public surplus. It can, however, increase $\dot{M}$ and consequently reduce the real return on holding money through inflation. Within the neoclassical framework, such an inflationary policy augments real capital accumulation in two ways. First, the increased public revenues from the inflation tax on cash balances can be deployed efficiently toward real capital accumulation within the public sector or through a functioning capital market. Second, through the substitution effect, private savers can be induced to acquire more "real" capital at the expense of real money, with their rate of saving out of private disposable income remaining about the same. In short, social saving rises as a proportion of aggregate income, and more of it is directed toward physical capital of uniform productivity.

The opportunity cost of this inflation is the reduced productivity of the economy caused by the decline in the input of real money balances. Yet if physical capital seems very scarce, the loss of transactions efficiency seems like a social cost well worth bearing as long as the inflation stops short of driving the economy to barter. Indeed, some authors have not even included real money as an input in the aggregate production function, and thus no productivity loss results from using the inflation tax to increase real accumulation![10]

Thus there is the paradox that, although a "first-best" policy calls for deflation under the full-liquidity rule, a second-best policy, which takes the capital scarcity and fiscal incapacity of poor countries into account, is one of inflation. No wonder less sophisticated development enthusiasts in Latin America and elsewhere have felt little academic restraint against pursuing inflationary policies as a response to capital scarcity.

Apart from the inflation issue, there is a purely logical difficulty in establishing a determinate demand for real cash balances within the neoclassical model. The transactions motive for holding money cannot exist if capital markets are perfect! With instantaneous and costless credit at the single going rate of interest on assets of all maturities (assumption 1, above) there would be no demand for cash balances if the real return on holding money is less than the return to physical capital. Automatic credit facilities everywhere would take care of even the day-to-day, hour-to-hour exchange of commodities. Alternatively, individuals could carry perfectly divisible physical capital in their pockets. There would be no need, therefore, to hold noninterest-bearing money as a medium of exchange. Money could retain its role as numeraire, but, when interest at the equilibrium rate is not paid to money holders, the demand to hold cash balances would be arbitrarily small. Essentially there is full liquidity without money.

A determinate demand for money requires imperfections in the capital market where there are risks of default and the rates of return on physical and on financial assets differ. In the less developed countries, individuals certainly do face upward-sloping and

10. Robert A. Mundell, "Inflation and Real Interest," *Journal of Political Economy*, Vol. 71 (June 1963), pp. 280–83; James Tobin, "Money and Economic Growth," *Econometrica*, Vol. 33 (October 1965), pp. 671–84; Duncan K. Foley, Karl Shell, and Miguel Sidrauski, "Optimal Fiscal and Monetary Policy and Economic Growth," *Journal of Political Economy*, Vol. 77 (July/August 1969), Pt. 2, pp. 698–719.

different supply curves for finance, with indivisibilities in, and restraints on, borrowing. Cash balances are needed to intermediate between income and expenditures, and the demand for money is a truly continuously increasing function of $d - \dot{P}^*$. Of course, these imperfections in capital markets also exist in advanced countries, albeit in less extreme forms. Their implications for monetary policy, however, can be sketched in sharpest relief in the underdeveloped context, as is done in Chapter 6.

## *Technical Note*

The purpose of this note is to sketch the basic model of David Levhari and Don Patinkin, which was used to derive the neoclassical investment function provided in the text. The same model generates the full-liquidity rule defining the level of real cash balances that is socially optimal.

There is a choice of convenience between viewing real money balances as a producers' good or as a consumers' good. To shorten the exposition here, money is treated only as an input into the aggregate production function; that is, it does not enter private utility functions directly and affects welfare only through increasing the flow of real goods and services available to individuals.

Reflecting this simplification and the neoclassical assumptions 1 through 4 listed in this chapter, the aggregate production function for the economy can be written:

$$(5\text{-}7) \qquad Y = G(K, L, M/P),$$

where $K$ is divisible physical capital of uniform productivity, $L$ is a homogeneous labor input, and $M/P$ is the real stock of money.

The quantity $Y$ is the real output of goods and services, some of which may be invested in the form of $K$. Money is physically productive, much like the stock of capital or the current flow of labor services, and indeed this is the source of the transactions demand for it. Hence, it is logical that money should also be treated as a productive input, even though it is costless to produce. If money is productive social wealth like physical capital, then increases in the real stock of money are a part of disposable income, $Y_D$, where

(5-8)  $\qquad Y_D = Y + d(M/P)/dt = Y + (\dot{M} - \dot{P})\, M/P.$

In neoclassical models, the savings function is rather arbitrarily specified as a given fraction, $0 < s < 1$, of disposable income, so that

(5-9)  $\qquad dK/dt = G(K, L, M/P) - (1 - s)Y_D.$

Substitute from equation 5-8 for $Y_D$ to get the investment function:

(5-10)  $\qquad dK/dt = sY + (s - 1)\,(\dot{M} - \dot{P})\, M/P.$

Since $s - 1 < 0$ and $\dot{M} - \dot{P} > 0$, we have the rather disconcerting result mentioned in the text that an increase in the real stock of money, $M/P$, may reduce the real rate of investment. Because the savings propensity is fixed and savings can be directed only toward real balances or toward physical capital, they are substitutes. The two are "competing assets" over the whole range of returns on holding money and real rates of return on physical assets.

Since money is socially costless to create, the government should induce private holders to expand $M/P$ until the marginal productivity of money, $\partial G/\partial(M/P)$, declines to zero. Money should not be economized on in any way. Since money competes with physical assets in the portfolios of savers, this policy implies that $\dot{M}$ should be manipulated until the rate of *deflation* equals the marginal physical product of capital if the nominal interest rate on deposits is zero. From our condition of portfolio equilibrium, equation 5-3 above, the full-liquidity rule implies that cash balances are expanded until the marginal convenience yield on money disappears:

(5-11)  $\qquad \partial G/\partial(M/P) = 0,$ and $\dot{P} = -r \equiv \partial G/\partial K.$

# 6

## The Demand for Money in Accumulating Capital: An Alternative View

IN RECONSIDERING HOW money enters the process of accumulating physical capital in poor countries, the relationships sketched in Chapter 4 can be carried forward intact. The price level continues to be determined by the demand for and supply of nominal money. Individuals still form expectations about future price movements—expectations that are highly influential in determining real cash balances actually held. The monetary authority determines the real return on holding money by controlling the rate of expansion in nominal cash balances, $\dot{M}$, and the nominal rate of return to the holders of money, $d$. What is changed, however, is the economy itself. We are now in the fragmented economic environment described in Chapter 2, and it remains to be shown what implications this fragmentation has for monetary theory and policy.

One obvious implication of imperfect capital markets is the increased importance of lending by banks, which can utilize money's peculiar attractiveness as an asset in an uncertain world in order to attract depositors. However, such an analysis requires an explicit model of real inputs supplied to the banking system, and of bank regulation. This is deferred to Chapters 7–9.

Instead, let us use initially the neoclassical assumption of outside fiat money—such as cash hidden under a mattress—which is virtually costless to produce, and rule out intermediation between savers and investors by banks or other financial institutions, such as insurance companies or pension funds. Then, with this self-imposed handicap, the essential complementarity between "owned" cash balances and real capital accumulation can be demonstrated through the demand function for holding money, rather than through the "seigniorage" associated with its issue. In this way, the contrast with neoclassical demand theory can be seen more readily.

The lack of organized finance in less developed countries and the inadequacy of government substitutes for financial processes (Chapter 3) seem to justify the following additional simplifying assumptions for purposes of model building:

*A.* All economic units are confined to self-finance, with no useful distinction to be made between savers (households) and investors (firms), according to the argument developed in Chapter 2. These firm–households do not borrow from, or lend to, each other.

*B.* The small size of firm–households implies that indivisibilities in investment are of considerable importance—as was shown in Figure 2-1.

*C.* The government does not participate directly in capital accumulation through the tax-expenditure process or by using seigniorage from money issue for capital formation. Revenues are used only to finance current government consumption.

Notice that assumptions *A* and *B*, above, reverse assumptions 1 and 2 of the neoclassical model, described in Chapter 5. *A* implies that cash balances are the only financial instruments available that can be accumulated or sold freely. *A* and *B* together imply that restraint on external borrowing inhibits individual enterprises from undertaking discrete investments that embody best-practice technologies. The result is widely dispersed rates of return on physical capital with a melange of firm–households operating at very different levels of efficiency in their use of money, as well as in their use of land and labor. In effect, the polar opposite of the neoclassical approach has been adopted here, and completely imperfect capital markets have been assumed.

*C* reverses assumption 5 and, in an extreme way, takes account of the fiscal constraints that are faced by most governments in poor countries. The government is frail in comparison to that of neo-classical philosopher-kings, who had unrestricted fiscal power. This limitation on capital accumulation by the government is consistent with an economy—perhaps largely agrarian—where investment opportunities are scattered widely in small firm–households. Since government fiscal action cannot affect aggregate capital accumulation directly, public policy is limited to the selection of the real return on holding money, $d - \dot{P}^*$, which does impinge on private investment, as is shown below.

## Complementarity between Money and Physical Capital

Suppose an individual saver-investor, being limited to self-finance, wants to purchase physical capital of a type that is different from his own output. (Only in purely subsistence agriculture would his own output be directly usable as a capital asset.) He may store inventories of his own output for eventual sale when the capital assets are acquired, or he may steadily accumulate cash balances for the same purpose. The degree to which he relies on one mode or the other will depend on the real return on holding money and the inconvenience of storing his own product. If $d - \dot{P}^*$ rises, he will use money more and his own inventories less as an efficient store of value.

Going further, assumption $B$ implies that a substantial agglomeration of purchasing power is concentrated at the particular point at which (or period over which) the investment is undertaken—whether it be in fixed assets, such as machinery, or even seed-fertilizer-pesticide packages of "working" capital for farmers. The average time interval between income and expenditures is longer in the case of investment than it is in the case of pure consumption. Correspondingly, the demand for real money balances will be strongly influenced by the propensity to save (invest). More precisely, *if the desired rate of capital accumulation (and hence private saving) increases at any given level of income, the average ratio of real cash balances to income will also increase.*

Because the above argument is central to the demonstration of complementarity between money and physical capital, a simple

FIGURE 6-1. *Alternative Time Profiles of Money-Holding for Consumption and Investment*

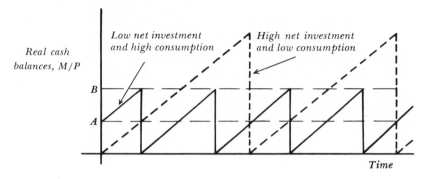

diagrammatic exposition seems in order. Figure 6-1 portrays alternative time profiles of the cash-balance holdings of two "typical" firm–households—one profile by a solid line and the other by a broken one. For simplicity, assume that income is received continuously at the same level in both firms through time, whereas disbursements are subject to indivisibilities that are measured by the vertical drops. The sum of these vertical drops must be equal for both firms if both have the same income, as in Figure 6-1.[1]

The propensity to undertake self-financed investments then is indicated by the size and spacing of the vertical drops. In particular, the solid line is the time profile for holding money when all or most income is devoted to consumption. Average holdings of cash balances at point *A* are quite low because of the relatively smooth profile of consumption expenditures. On the other hand, the dashed line represents a flow of expenditures devoted mainly to a sequence of investments. The greater lag between income and disbursements associated with "lumpiness" in investment leads to higher average cash balances—denoted by *B*—in the investment-oriented enterprise. Average cash balance holdings, therefore, are positively related to the propensity to invest (save) under the formal constraint that all investments are "self-financed"—as indeed some always are in practice.

These complex time profiles can be incorporated into a function describing the *average* demand to hold money, as is indicated by

1. The author is indebted to Hayne Leland of Stanford University for clarifying this analysis.

points $A$ and $B$ in Figure 6-1. The function $L$ in equation 6-1 includes the investment/income ratio, $I/Y$, as one of the determinants of the real stock of money, $M/P$; and hence $L$ incorporates the demand for money arising directly from the process of capital accumulation itself. The conventional transactions motive for holding money is still captured by current income, $Y$; and, of course, the real return on holding money also enters $L$ explicitly—with its variance or instability left implicit. The money-demand function is

$$(6\text{-}1) \qquad (M/P)^D = L(Y, I/Y, d - \dot{P}^*).$$

From the analysis above, all the partial derivatives of $L$ are positive. In particular, $\partial L/\partial(I/Y) > 0$ so as to reflect the basic complementarity between money and physical capital in fragmented economies.

In contrast, $I/Y$ does not even enter the neoclassical money-demand function, as was represented by $H$ in equation 5-1. The conventional approach is to use $r$—*the* real return to physical capital—in the money-demand function in place of $I/Y$. However, this conventional approach is of limited usefulness in the underdeveloped world, where actual rates of return vary greatly—both marginally and intramarginally. It is misleading to assume that there is a single real rate of return that is also the uniform opportunity cost of holding money. Money, like everything else, is used with varying marginal efficiency.

Assume instead an average return to capital, $\bar{r}$, with a given dispersion around it measuring the variable productivity of capital among firm–households. Now consider exogenous changes in the environment that could raise $\bar{r}$, such as opening an economy to foreign trade or introducing a "green revolution" in agriculture. Then desired investment would increase as $\bar{r}$ was raised. With this carefully limited interpretation of exogenously determined changes in $r$, a more familiar money-demand function is obtained:

$$(6\text{-}2) \qquad (M/P)^D = L(Y, \bar{r}, d - \dot{P}^*),$$

where $\partial L/\partial Y > 0$, $\partial L/\partial \bar{r} > 0$, and $\partial L/\partial(d - \dot{P}^*) > 0$.

The key point here is the complementarity relationship where $\partial L/\partial \bar{r} > 0$, in contrast to the situation where $\partial H/\partial r < 0$ in the neoclassical model. A rise in the average rate of return to physical capital *increases* desired real cash-balance holdings because the rise is associated with an increase in the investment/income ratio. (It would not be true if the rise in $\bar{r}$ were associated with a fall in the aggregate propensity to save.) In contrast, the traditional portfolio approach treats money and physical capital as substitutable forms of wealth-holding in a quite static sense where the accumulation process per se is ignored. However, if money is viewed as a conduit through which accumulation takes place—rather than as a competing asset—the demand for money rises *pari passu* with the productivity of physical capital.

This complementarity works both ways; the conditions of money supply have a first-order impact on decisions to save and invest—again unlike the neoclassical model. In particular, *if the real return on holding money increases, so will self-financed investment over a significant range of investment opportunities*. The increased desirability of holding cash balances reduces the opportunity cost of saving internally for the eventual purchase of capital goods from outside the firm–household. The financial "conduit" for capital accumulation is thereby enlarged.

The sources of the increased attractiveness of holding money are several. In some relatively primitive economies, simply opening up new physical facilities for deposit banking will increase the demand for money. In both primitive and more mature economies, a reduction in the rate of inflation and/or variance of the price level can increase the demand for real cash balances. Alternatively, the nominal interest rate on deposits can be raised. In all of these cases, the resulting increase in the real return on money can raise sharply investment-savings propensities because of the importance of money as a store of value. In contrast, $d - \dot{P}^*$ does not directly affect the propensity to save within the neoclassical model because all firms have perfect access to external sources of finance at a uniform real rate of return, even in periods of high and unstable inflation.

This complementarity between money and physical capital is reflected in the investment function, $F$, given by equation 6-3.[2]

2. On a steady-state balanced growth path one would eventually expect a steady $I/Y$ to yield a steady $K/Y$, where $K$ is the stock of physical capital. However, our long run is not that long.

(6-3)                    $I/Y = F(\bar{r}, d - \dot{P}^*)$,

where $\partial F/\partial \bar{r} > 0$, and $\partial F/\partial (d - \dot{P}^*) \lessgtr 0$.

Although the "conduit" effect of money has been emphasized, the traditional "competing-asset" effect between money and physical capital can prevail in particular circumstances. The mixture of the two yields the ambiguous sign of the second partial derivative of equation 6-3. Can one generalize about when one effect or the other would be dominant? Such a generalization would help determine the optimal return on holding money to be set by the monetary authorities.

## Optimization within the New Model

Our poor fragmented economy is inherently less tractable than its highly efficient neoclassical counterpart, and it is not possible to draw elegant general-equilibrium conclusions comparable to the golden and full-liquidity rules. One can, however, proceed on a partial-equilibrium basis by taking current levels of income as given. Then assume that the prevailing capital scarcity drives the government to set the real return on holding money so as to *maximize* the rate of self-financed investment by the average firm–household. This is the only avenue open to official policy under assumption *C*, above, which precludes capital accumulation by the government.

Where is this maximum likely to occur? The conduit effect of money for encouraging investment is particularly important when monetization in the form of owned cash balances is limited—as when the real return to money holders is very unfavorable, possibly to the point of being made highly negative by inflation. The process of self-financed investment is correspondingly constricted by the small size and high costs (to investors) of the monetary system. Then a higher real return on holding money relaxes the saving–investment bottleneck by enlarging $M/P$. On the other hand, once $d - \dot{P}^*$ rises toward the best marginal and intramarginal returns to be earned on self-financed investments, the competing-asset effect becomes dominant and *reduces* the aggregate flow of investment. That is, when the real return on holding money is already high, further increases in this return may induce net portfolio substitution away from the accumulation of physical capital toward cash balances. The latter become attractive as earning assets in their own right. Both effects are present at any one time, and the relative importance of one or the other is summarized in Figure 6-2 below, which illustrates equation 6-3, with $\bar{r}$ held constant.

The authorities set the real return on money, which is measured on the horizontal axis of Figure 6-2. The interval $AB$ is one of complementarity between $M/P$ and $I/Y$ because of the conduit effect. For returns on money greater than $B$, however, the competing-asset effect begins to reduce investment. Hence, a return on money equal to $B$ maximizes the rate of self-financed investment and is the rate of return that a monetary authority should seek in the absence of other avenues for capital accumulation.

Can anything more be said about this optimum level of the real return on holding money? It is highly desirable socially to bar investments whose internal rates of return are actually negative, even though such investments as stores of value may be privately undertaken if $d - \dot{P}^* < 0$. The competing-asset effect acts favorably to constrain social waste if the return on money is kept positive because individuals will not hold nonmonetary assets whose return is less than that earned on highly liquid cash balances. It is

FIGURE 6-2. *Effect of the Real Return on Holding Money on Self-Financed Investment*

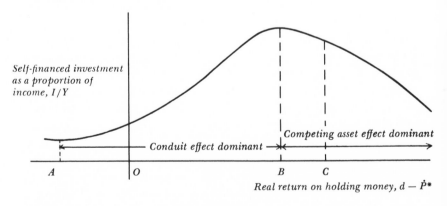

Source: Derived from equation 6-3, discussed in text.

impossible to deduce this result from the neoclassical model, where all physical capital is of uniform and presumably positive productivity, whether or not the real return on holding money is negative.

The same point can be made more forcefully by noting how other goods might substitute for money as a store of value or as an inflation hedge. If the real return on holding money is low or negative, a significant proportion of the physical capital of the economy will be embodied in inventories of finished and semi-finished goods that are not used directly for production or consumption. A small farmer may keep unduly large rice inventories as the embodiment of his savings—a portion of which the rats eat every year. Alternatively, a wealthy member of some urban enclave may build an unusually elaborate house, which he hopes will also maintain its value under inflation. A businessman might deliberately "over-invest" in plant capacity or in certain stocks of raw materials, relative to his current operating needs. A rise in the real return on holding money, therefore, can result in a large once-and-for-all improvement in aggregate output when this low productivity "capital" is put to more efficient uses as money becomes more attractive as a store of value. Going beyond this immediate impact of increasing $d - \dot{P}^*$, however, a growing economy will gain continuously by not having to direct new social savings year after year toward these nonproductive forms of fixed or working capital. In summary, the quality of the capital stock is directly and positively related to the real return on holding money.

There is an index number problem in measuring investment because of differential rates of return to physical capital. $I/Y$ in equation 6-3 has been defined simply as the proportion of the income of the firm–household that goes into asset formation. If there is a distinct improvement in the quality of the stock of physical capital as a result of a rise in the real return on holding money, it is conceivable that the social optimum may be to the right of the maximum investment flow—say at point $C$ rather than point $B$ in Figure 6-2. However, this result would require more explicit assumptions about the "technology" of investment. In contrast, a highly negative real return on money could drive investment to some low level with a highly inefficient physical embodiment.

The intramarginal or discontinuous nature of investment opportunities available to each firm–household suggests another related argument for maintaining high returns to the holders of cash balances. Poverty makes it difficult for individuals to accumulate the funds needed to finance these lump-sum investments, but a high rate of return earned on accumulating owned cash balances reduces this difficulty. Disinvesting in traditional techniques and planning for quantum investments in new technologies can then proceed according to the analysis in Chapter 2. For example, a small farmer may well find it feasible to save for four or five years in the form of money in order to invest eventually in a new tube well for irrigating his crops. If he were confined to small annual investments at the margin because money was unattractive as a store of value, at best he could make only minor improvements in his old "dry" farming technology.

The importance of these intramarginal investments means that the average return to physical capital in the economy as a whole need *not* fall as the financial-monetary system becomes more efficient and the total volume of investment increases. Rather, the average return to new investment may remain substantially above $d - \dot{P}^*$, even when this return on holding money is raised. This "gap" is due to the indivisible nature of investment opportunities coupled with a high premium on current consumption in a poverty-stricken world. Fortunately, the traditional preoccupation of academic economists with diminishing returns from capital formation, beginning with the great classical authors, such as David Ricardo, and carried on in the work of modern neoclassical growth theorists, can be dispensed with once the nature of financial restraint on individual enterprises in the underdeveloped economy is taken into account.

However, this simple monetary system based on self-finance is still unduly limiting even when ideally managed. There is a definite upper limit to the optimal return on holding money, as indicated by point $B$ (or possibly $C$) in Figure 6-2. The return at $B$ may be well below that earned on many potential investments that could be undertaken if banks were active lenders. Self-finance constrains the monetary authorities to setting a real rate of return on holding money substantially below the return to be earned on the best intramarginal investments in physical capital in some firm–households, because the competing-asset effect of high cash balances reduces the flow of lower-return investments that are closer to the margin in other enterprises. Hence, there is a definite role for lending by financial institutions to break the confines of self-finance and "pool" savings more efficiently—a role that is explored more fully in Chapters 7–9. But even under self-finance, the optimal real return to the holders of money is much higher than traditional monetary theory suggests.

## *Nonmonetary Financing and Complementarity*

Reliance on self-finance is a reasonable working hypothesis in many less developed countries. However, village moneylenders, agricultural cooperatives, various urban curb markets, and inter-firm trade credit do exist and are sometimes important, even though they operate at very short term and high cost. Their existence need not upset our basic theme of complementarity between money and physical capital, because of the interpersonal uncertainty, which was analyzed in Chapter 2. On the contrary, the increased monetary liquidity of potential borrowers due to a higher return on holding money can reduce the risk that they will default. Hence, higher real cash balances provide security for potential outside investors that encourages direct lending. Figure 6-3 shows such direct financing augmenting the flow of self-financed investment for an individual firm–household whose investment now exceeds its own saving.

In Figure 6-3, total investment rises initially through its self-financed and externally financed components, as $d - \dot{P}*$ is increased. The widening of the shaded area shows these increases in the flow of direct lending by outside investors with specialized investment knowledge in the enterprise under consideration. Lenders see their risk reduced because of the greater monetary liquidity of the borrower and because the borrower's self-financed *equity* is augmented, which improves leverage. Lenders become more willing to provide resources to enterprises that do finance some of their own internal investment. Nevertheless, a sufficient rise in the return on holding money eventually makes the competing-asset effect dominant—both from the saver's and from the investor's point of view. Hence, the authorities remain constrained

FIGURE 6-3. *Effect of the Real Return on Holding Money on Self-Financed and Externally-Financed Investment*

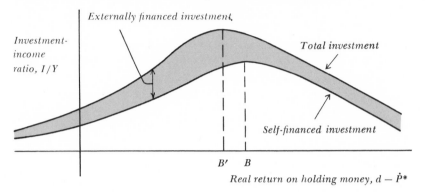

in the total amount of physical investment that they can encourage in this manner.

As with self-financed investments, the "quality" of direct financing can also improve as the return on money increases. As long as real cash balances are low, direct finance itself will take forms closely associated with barter. For example, in subsistence agriculture, sharecropping may be quite important. Payoffs are specified in terms of that portion of the output of the producing firm—household that is directly usable by potential creditors, as is illustrated by the Chilean case in Chapter 7. With increased monetization, however, finance can be specified more flexibly in terms of money, and the number of potential lenders is increased. Trade credit becomes practical, as do more general loans coming directly from savers with the requisite information on the risk they are taking in investing in someone else's enterprise. The efficiency of direct finance grows with the real return on holding money—particularly if that return has been very low.

## Policy Implications of the New Approach: A Summary

Our model of monetary processes in an economy with imperfect capital markets can be usefully contrasted with the neoclassical alternative summarized in Chapter 5.

• The quality of the capital stock (average rate of return) is positively related to the real return on holding money.

• The demands for stocks of cash balances and physical capital are complementary over a range where the conduit effect dominates the competing-asset effect.

• Private saving (investment) is quite sensitive to the real return on holding money and its stability.

• There is a determinate optimal real return on money that is likely to be significantly greater than zero and a presumption that inflation is a poor way to deal with the scarcity of real capital.

• Indivisibilities are such that investment can be increased—using appropriate financial techniques—without diminishing returns.

A comprehensive discussion of monetary management is deferred until the conditions of money supply are specified more completely. It is clear, however, that money is important. It is also clear that one can be optimistic about the favorable impact of monetary reform on economic development through the release of financial restraint on capital formation. The dismal science is less dismal without diminishing returns. Correspondingly, monetary mismanagement resulting in high inflation may be much more damaging than prevailing theory would suggest.

Apart from the control of inflation over long periods of time, the direction of monetary management that is suggested by this theoretical schema may differ from the direction suggested by short-run Keynesian theory. Suppose there is an exogenous improvement in real rates of return to physical investment such as accompanies a green revolution in agriculture. At any given income level, the resulting increases in the propensities to save and invest will generate an increased demand for real money balances. Correspondingly, to avoid deflation the authorities should permit the nominal supply of money to increase. In contrast, a Keynesian model might call for a contraction in nominal money to balance the "inflationary" impact of the investment boom.[3]

---

3. Indubitably, John Maynard Keynes himself was more sophisticated than current Keynesian theory. After the *General Theory*, he noted that an increase in *ex ante* or planned investment activity would temporarily increase the demand for money. However, once plans were realized, the "unusual" demand would disappear. (See "The Ex Ante Theory of the Rate of Interest," *Economic Journal*, Vol. 47 [December 1937], p. 667.) This *ex ante* effect is certainly present in our model, but there is an additional permanent effect of an increase in the $I/Y$ ratio when plans are realized. The latter was not recognized by Keynes because he assumed that the bond market would be the continuing source of primary finance, rather than the accumulation and spending of owned cash balances.

# 7

---

# Financial Repression and Inflation

---

THE ASSUMPTION OF SELF-FINANCE used in Chapter 6 was a helpful analytical device for showing the essential complementarity between physical capital and real money balances—even low-cost fiat money, whose issue was not associated with the expansion of bank credit to investors. "Self-finance" describes reasonably accurately the situation in underdeveloped economies, where there is no operating capital market. Yet full liberalization requires breaking the confines of self-finance and channeling external funds to large and small investors who can earn high marginal and intramarginal rates of return. Hence a case can be made for a more costly monetary system based on extensive bank lending, to exploit more fully the ability of money and near-monies to attract savings in an uncertain world.

But organized banking has a sorry record in penetrating the economic hinterland of less developed countries (LDCs), in serving rural areas in general, and in serving small borrowers in particular. Bank credit remains a financial appendage of certain enclaves: exclusively licensed import activities, specialized large-scale mineral exports, highly protected manufacturing, large international corporations, and various government agencies, such as coffee marketing boards or publicly controlled utilities. Even ordinary government deficits on current account frequently preempt the limited lending resources of the deposit banks. Financing of the rest of the economy must be met from the meager resources of moneylenders, pawnbrokers, and cooperatives. It is this phenomenon that I call "financial repression."

The failure of banks to earn high equilibrium rates of return from their privileged borrowers is reflected back in an unduly low return to depositors—one that may well be negative in real terms if inflation is at all significant. Scarce capital is underpriced by the banks although not by the moneylenders. It is hardly surprising that savers respond to low real returns by reducing their holdings of money and near-monies far below what might be considered socially optimal; and, of course, outstanding bank credit is reduced commensurately. The surprisingly low ratios of money to gross national product to be found in the less developed countries are documented more fully in Chapter 8.

An increase in the efficiency of bank lending is, therefore, a necessary condition for enlarging the real size of the monetary system and for alleviating financial repression. In this chapter, the historically "poor" performance of organized bank lending is related to regulated interest ceilings and collateral requirements. Then it is shown how the resulting financial repression can be aggravated by a typical cycle of inflation and attempted deflation, as exemplified by the experiences of Brazil in the mid-1960s and Chile in the late 1950s. Finally, techniques for deflating successfully—in the sense of avoiding a contraction in income and employment—are contrasted with "orthodox" monetary prescriptions.

## Banking Restraint and Its Consequences for Traditional Credit Markets

In the colonial period, organized banking served mainly expatriates who were engaged in developing exports of raw materials.[1] Indeed, insofar as indigenous individuals in the colony participated in the process of bank intermediation, they were depositors rather than borrowers. Funds would be channeled to banks—controlled largely in, say, London—which then would reinvest funds with borrowers whose collateral and reputations were known to

1. Jonathan V. Levin, *The Export Economies: Their Patterns of Development in Historical Perspective* (Harvard University Press, 1960), pp. 144–54.

the overseas bankers. Tea plantations and rubber estates in the Far East were developed by Europeans with overseas banking connections and access to direct finance, even though their technical skill may have been no greater than that of non-Europeans. Entrepreneurship in the indigenous economy was allowed to languish without significant financial support. The situation in Egypt has been described by Eshag and Kamal:[2]

> At the turn of the century some three-quarters of a million farmers representing over 80 per cent of Egypt's landowners were small-holders in the sense that their lands consisted of lots of less than 5 feddans (1 feddan = 1.038 acres). Most, if not all, of these farmers had no access to credit on normal commercial terms from the country's real estate and commercial banks. Real estate banks, whose minimum loans were fixed at £E400, catered exclusively for the long-term needs of estate owners who were able to offer adequate collateral security for loans. As the market value of the average holding in the under 5 feddans size-group was well below £E400, no small-holder could qualify for these loans. The Government had tried, but in vain, to persuade the leading real estate bank in 1896 to reduce the minimum level of its advances from £E400 to £E100, an amount which would have been just below the value of the average peasant holding.
>
> Commercial banks were mainly concerned with financing the principal export crop, cotton, by advancing short-term loans to big landlords, merchants and exporters; but they were unwilling to undertake small credit transactions with the mass of small cultivators. Some of the funds advanced by the banks were passed down to small cotton growers, but the interest charged by the intermediaries was invariably much higher than the statutory maximum of 9 per cent charged by the commercial banks.

With independence and the development of national banking in LDCs, this overseas colonization of the banks has virtually disappeared. It has been replaced, however, by a very similar "neo-colonial" banking system, where favored private and official borrowers still absorb the limited finance available at low real rates of interest, which are often far below the opportunity cost of scarce capital. Again, the mass of small farmers and indigenous urban industry remain financially "repressed," although they own a significant proportion of the deposits on which the expansion of

2. Eprime Eshag and M. A. Kamal, "A Note on the Reform of the Rural Credit System in U.A.R. (Egypt)," in *Bulletin* of the Oxford University Institute of Economics and Statistics, Vol. 29 (May 1967), p. 97.

bank credit to the favored enclaves is based. Real rates of interest may be even further out of line in this neocolonial system as compared to the colonial one, even if unrequited seigniorage is no longer accruing to some foreign financial center.

For example, moneylenders in rural Ethiopia are known to receive interest at 100 to 200 percent a year for providing loans of as little as $50 to $100. Poor farmers need capital to bridge the gap between the time when they grow or harvest their crops and when they actually market them. Unfortunately, few agricultural loans are made by the organized banking system; and facilities for holding deposits offer limited physical accessibility in rural areas, and rates of interest paid on deposits are low. This dearth of organized banking on both the deposit and lending sides raises the cost of financing inventories of agricultural produce, making it high for traders as well as farmers, and ensures marked seasonal variation in grain prices. Thus farmers who store their crops may receive much greater net proceeds than do their more poverty-stricken colleagues, who effectively sell at or before the harvest by pledging their crops or by borrowing.

Despite this revealed scarcity and productivity of unsophisticated rural investment, the standard nominal lending rate to protected manufacturing activity, and real estate promotion (such as hotel building) is 8 or 9 percent in Ethiopia's few urban areas. Importers borrow at rates closer to 6 percent. Together with the government, these borrowers absorb virtually all of the banks' lending resources. The legal interest rate ceiling on bank loans is 12 percent, although little lending takes place at that rate; and the maximum interest rate on two-year time deposits is 7 percent a year, the average nominal interest rate on deposits being much lower than this. These huge interest differentials between organized banking and informal "rural"[3] credit in Ethiopia are not unusually great relative to those in other LDCs. Inflation is moderate, and thus Ethiopian interest rates are at least significantly positive in real terms, unlike the rates in many Latin American countries. Nevertheless, the disparity between rates charged in urban enclaves and those in rural areas—the latter containing 80 to 90 percent of the population—is startling if not uncommon.

3. The term "rural" refers not only to subsistence agriculture, but also to all "nonenclave" economic activity, including small-scale manufacturing and services.

Rural moneylending and the extension of trade credit through village stores offer only a partial substitute for organized bank finance. From a sample survey of traditional credit markets in rural Chile, Charles Nisbet has estimated that only 30 percent of the total rural population are clients of state financial institutions, reform agencies, and private commercial banks.[4] Most of the others use informal credit markets, as do some of the clients of the banks.

> Additionally, the past policies of private and state lending institutions have contributed to the maintenance of imperfect competition in the informal credit market and to the accompanying high rates of interest. Until 1959 there was no important institutional source of credit for the "low income sectors," and as late as 1964 only 4 percent of the total credit extended by private and state lending institutions went to farmers within this sector. It is precisely the low income farm operators who negotiate most frequently with lenders [in] the informal credit market. Thus, historically, commercial lenders have been free from competition and have been assisted indirectly in maintaining their yearly expropriation of monopoly profits.[5]

The lack of penetration of organized bank lending into the rural economy and into small-scale urban industry has been corroborated by U Tun Wai in a massive empirical study of those LDCs, for which data were available.[6]

Important as they are, the traditional or informal credit markets are quite inadequate for reducing dispersion in real rates of interest for the majority of the rural population. Nisbet found that, on an average, any randomly chosen farmer had access to only two sources of credit, say a moneylender and a village store. This fragmentation permits the exercise of monopoly or duopoly power, which can be exploitive and inevitably leads to highly differentiated rates of interest. "With inflation removed from interest rates on currency loans . . . most commercial lenders emerge with positive rates ranging from 27 percent to 360 percent, with an annual mean rate of 82 percent."[7] About half of these loans went for consumption purposes.

4. Charles Nisbet, "Interest Rates and Imperfect Competition in the Informal Credit Market of Rural Chile," *Economic Development and Cultural Change*, Vol. 16 (October 1967), p. 73.

5. *Ibid.*, p. 85.

6. U Tun Wai, "Interest Rates Outside the Organized Money Markets of Underdeveloped Countries," International Monetary Fund, *Staff Papers*, Vol. 6 (November 1957), pp. 80–142.

7. Nisbet, "Interest Rates and Imperfect Competition," p. 76.

In the examples given above, usury ceilings on the interest rates charged on bank loans have emasculated the ability and willingness of commercial banks to serve small-scale borrowers of all classes. A maximum interest rate of 10 percent does not begin to cover the administrative costs and potential default risks inherent in small-scale lending. Hence, the great mass of small firm–households is driven into the arms of moneylenders. In addition to restricting the overall volume of bank lending, the interest ceiling ensures that the trickle of available finance flows to completely safe borrowers whose reputation is known or whose collateral is relatively riskless. Or worse, the great excess demand for loans allows allocations to be contingent on political or "establishment" connections. Importers holding exclusive licenses, or the largest landowners, or various government agencies are likely to be the beneficiaries. Since these "good" risks are frequently individuals with large visible incomes and asset holdings, loans made to them at low regulated rates of interest tend to exacerbate the already skewed distribution of income.

Paradoxically, cheap credit in a populist sense may not benefit the little man at all. Quite the contrary. It may effectively prevent him from competing for long-term finance from the organized banking system, and as a result he is confined to getting month-to-month credit from the village storekeeper.

These interest-rate restrictions may have resulted from attempts to regulate the *monopoly power* of a banking system that is indeed likely to be highly concentrated in a small economy. But even a 10 percent interest rate ceiling on loans can provide a rather comfortable margin between interest rates on demand deposits set at zero and time deposit rates set at, say, 5 percent. Bankers usually do not feel compelled to complain about the overall structure of interest rate regulation, even though the flow of loans and deposits remains small in real terms. Even regulated monopolists can lead rather pleasant, quiet lives!

In Chile during the 1950s, when price inflation averaged 40 percent a year and reached a maximum of 80 percent in 1955, the nominal discount rate used by the central bank ranged between 4.5 and 6 percent a year—with the loan rate to favored customers of the commercial banks not far above that. These highly negative real rates of interest provided extraordinarily heavy subsidies to various industrial and commercial users of bank credit. Nonetheless, ceilings on nominal rates of interest were themselves rationalized as an antimonopoly device:

> The view prevails in Chile generally, but especially within the ranks of the principal borrowers, that the "monopolistic" banking system would, with free interest rates, use its power to maximize "profits" regardless of the impact on aggregate economic activity. To protect the general public from the unemployment that might result from this present-day "usury," it is argued that controls on interest rates are essential. Thus, despite the fact that the government could presumably place its debt with the Central Bank, and continue to collect the "inflation tax" with higher interest rates, it has acceded to the demand for controls on the interest rate. This policy has persisted despite the fact that the government's control over the directorate of the Central Bank is virtually complete. Presumably the persistence of this policy is simply another reflection of the fact that the larger units in the industrial and commercial sector have become dependent upon the "inflation" subsidy to a degree that Radical, Independent, and Right governments have all felt compelled to recognize and accept.[8]

## Common Policy Responses to Financial Repression

How do public authorities respond to the evident imbalance in the availability and cost of credit throughout the economy? One response is to extend the usury restrictions—ceilings on interest charged by banks—to rural moneylenders and grain merchants. Such policies can indeed drive the money changers from the temple so that the trickle of rural finance dries up altogether. The result is even greater fragmentation in the returns to capital and more instability in crop prices. In Chile, as in most of the less developed countries, usury laws existed and were largely evaded, but they added to the costs of operating in the informal credit market.

Governments may tolerate moneylending at high rates of interest but try to mitigate some of its unfortunate social effects. The default rate on exorbitant loans can be substantial. When land is pledged as collateral—as it often is—lenders assume control of farm properties so that the distribution of land ownership is skewed

---

8. Tom E. Davis, "Eight Decades of Inflation in Chile, 1879–1959: A Political Interpretation," *Journal of Political Economy*, Vol. 71 (August 1963), pp. 395–96.

further. Such "negative" land reform can lead to the rise of a landless peasantry. Public authorities frequently respond either by prohibiting the pledging of land or by preventing foreclosure by the lender.

In Malaya, for example, the acquisition of substantial blocs of land from defaulting Malay farmers led to the passage of the Malay Land Reservations Act. Because the moneylenders were largely Chinese or Indian, the act essentially prohibited them from assuming title to the property on which they did foreclose. Of course, access to finance became even more limited when the Malay farmers found that they could no longer put their land up as collateral to secure loans. A similar phenomenon was described in Chapter 3 with respect to the Mexican ejidos, which are land parcels that cannot be resold. Such social restraint on foreclosure is commonplace. When strong, it turns every farmer into an unsecured borrower, raises the cost of external finance, and generally fragments the capital market even further. The problem of providing collateral will always exist, but it becomes more critical when interest rates on loans are so high that the probability of default is substantial.

Another "solution" to the problem of channeling finance to small farmers—although it is not always recognized as a solution— is for the government to hold grain inventories and set crop prices. Essentially, the carrying of inventories is thrown into the public domain, which occasionally can be useful if price instability is particularly great. However, capital is still scarce, and public inventories have to be financed from the fiscally pressed exchequer. Moreover, experience in advanced and in less developed countries suggests that authorities come under tremendous pressure to set prices either too high in response to some farm groups or too low in response to urban pressure to keep the cost of "wage goods" down. Farm-price stabilization programs still do not directly help the individual farmer to tailor optimally his own access to external finance, the need for which was indicated in the Fisherian analysis in Chapter 2. Hence, such programs remain "second-best" solutions to the underlying capital constraint.

Public inventory and marketing control can be carried to extremes where the government essentially expropriates all crop proceeds and allocates credit and other agricultural inputs on a nonprice basis. This seems to have been the outcome of a series of land reforms carried on in Egypt since 1952.

The more difficult problem of ensuring that the poorer peasants, who were in greatest need of rescue from private money-lenders, would receive adequate help could not, however, be solved so easily. The solution of this problem required a wholesale transformation of the land tenure system and of the production and marketing organisations. This transformation which was responsible for the establishment of "supervised co-operatives" took place gradually; it started in 1952 and was barely completed by 1965. . . .

Its success was such that the co-operatives had become the sole suppliers of agricultural credit, and co-operative membership was compulsory for all farmers.

These measures, together with a further unorthodox measure—the abolition of interest on co-operative loans in 1961—resulted in a rapid expansion of credit to agriculture.

In this régime, where the authorities take actual possession of the farmers' crops and are left in charge of selling them and receiving the proceeds, farmers' poverty ceases to be an obstacle to their being advanced credit. As long as the value of a farmer's crops covers the loans made to him, the authorities run little risk of losing money in their credit operations. . . .

Under this system, loans in kind—seeds, fertilisers, etc.—are made to each farmer according to the area of the farm and the type of crop planted. On the other hand, the amount of cash loans allocated to each farmer is determined by reference to his cash outlays in production.[9]

The Egyptian farm policy is certainly one way of providing small farmers with some of the advantages inherent in having access to agricultural credit. It runs the danger, however, of throwing out the baby with the bathwater. Not only may crop prices be mis-specified, but there is a regression away from a monetary economy to a barter one. Farm produce is traded directly for certain inputs (in kind) whose quantities are determined by the government. This policy involves obvious elements of coercion. It also reduces the alternatives available for decision makers; for example, a farmer who wants to borrow a lot of credit this year but none in succeeding years cannot do so. From a broader point of view, the provision of credit at a zero rate of interest probably makes it all but impossible to reward savers—bank depositors—with a rate of return that reflects the great scarcity of capital. Hence, cheap credit for certain farmers probably accentuates financial repression elsewhere in the economy—unless real finance is heavenly manna left behind in the desert by the Children of Israel.

## *A Preferred Strategy for Overcoming Repression*

There appears to be no economical substitute for expanding the role of organized finance in small-scale lending to indigenous entrepreneurs in either rural or urban areas. However, such a course of action is not costless. The detailed information required from bank loan officers can be expensive in skilled resources. Risk is high, and assured collateral may not be available. Indeed, one would expect that replacing the services of well informed moneylenders would be expensive.

> The moneylender and village store owner have intimate personal knowledge of the borrower's circumstances. He [the moneylender] knows the size of the borrower's farm, the number of animals he owns, the output of the farm last year, his outstanding debts, the degree of his entrepreneurial skills, etc. This information is common knowledge to most people within the area, since the residents are socially and economically interdependent; however, the informal commercial lenders make it their business to mentally catalog and keep current all such data, to minimize risks.[10]

Hence, one would expect equilibrium interest rates charged by banks to rural and other small-scale borrowers to be substantial in order to reflect lending costs accurately. Nevertheless, *real* rates of interest of 15 to 25 percent can probably be charged in agricultural and other small-scale lending so as to be profitable for the banks as well as for the borrowers. These rates would be high enough to divert funds from low-yield investments in urban enclaves but still dramatically undercut some extremely high real rates of interest charged in traditional credit markets. Needless to say, high and unstable inflation makes it much more difficult for organized banking—dependent on money as a numeraire—to compete commercially. In Chile, inflation actually forces traditional lenders to demand repayment *in kind* in 50 percent of the loans Nisbet sampled.

---

10. Nisbet, "Interest Rates and Imperfect Competition," p. 81.

In addition to reaching vigorously for rural borrowers directly, on occasion the banks may save considerable administrative expense by working through traditional institutions, such as farm cooperatives. On a limited experimental basis, Ethiopia set up a rural development corporation—exempt from interest-rate restrictions—which received loans from a savings bank at 8 percent and in turn lent the money to a rural cooperative at 12 percent, which parceled out loans among its members at 17 percent.[11] Surprisingly there were no defaults, and all loans were repaid through the various layers on schedule. Needless to say, there was tremendous excess demand for rural loans at the 17 percent rate.

Like cooperatives, the moneylenders have valuable "inside" information that may usefully be mobilized by legalizing their operations through the removal of usury restrictions and by permitting them to expand their credit base by bank borrowing. At least in Chile these two measures would seem substantially to broaden competition in the traditional credit markets.

> There are three primary reasons why moneylenders operate on a small scale and do not compete with each other. First, the moneylenders do not have detailed knowledge of a broad market, so their type of business demands a small-scale operation which offers [operates under] continuous excess demand. Second, because their activities are illegal, they minimize the probability of encounters with legal authorities by restricting their operations geographically in number of clients and volume of credit. The illegality aspect and the separate client market discourage them from competing with a nearby moneylender. Lastly, the moneylenders are principally farmers, whose lending activities do not represent more than 50 percent of their annual gross income. Therefore, unlike the village stores, they lack the capital base to carry on large-scale lending.[12]

Alternatively, a rapidly expanding banking system may even exploit the experience of former moneylenders by making them loan officers, as has been the case in some countries. Of course, this would preclude their authorizing loans for themselves!

Nevertheless, the main burden of ensuring that there is uniformity in borrowing rates and that competition is broadly based rests with direct bank lending. Banks can be organized to operate competitively or to simulate competitive lending and deposit

---

11. I am indebted to C. P. Cacho of the International Bank for Reconstruction and Development for this information.

12. Nisbet, "Interest Rates and Imperfect Competition," p. 83.

practices, even if the banking structure remains highly concentrated. In most developing countries, this requires a major increase in the willingness *and* ability of banks to purchase primary securities from final investors at rates of interest that reflect the general scarcity of capital and the peculiar administrative costs of serving each class of borrower. Equally important, the term for which such finance is made available must be greatly lengthened. Loans at high interest rates but in larger quantity and for longer terms can produce the technological leap-frogging effect analyzed in more detail within our Fisherian model, described in Chapter 2, above. The prevailing policy of providing "cheap" bank credit to a few favored borrowers or small dribbles to a larger number—whether in the government sector or outside it—would have to be discontinued.

This preferred strategy of high real rates of interest—where real finance is plentiful at those rates—may be nearly impossible in an economy with high and unstable inflation. Uncertainty and the desire to avoid risk may make nominal rates of interest that incorporate the expected future price inflation look too high to borrowers and too low to depositors. The former don't want to be trapped with high fixed nominal interest-rate commitments if inflation should slow down, while the latter don't want to be wiped out if there is an unanticipated acceleration in the upward price movement. Hence, none but financial commitments of the shortest term can be established.

Can price inflation be accepted and then offset by appropriate adjustments in nominal rates of interest? Indexing of interest rates by the banking authority so as to maintain their real value as inflation proceeds is itself expensive, and it is difficult to define a suitable commodity numeraire. Adjusting nominal interest rates to reflect movements in some commodity price index may, however, be better than no protection against unexpected price movement. With moderate inflation—say less than 15 percent a year—nominal rates of interest can be raised by 10 or 15 percentage points to reflect expected price movements fairly accurately without depositors and borrowers feeling undue risk—as is shown in Chapter 8. Nevertheless believable stability in the price level is greatly to be desired; and the tricky problem of deflating without exacerbating financial repression is discussed below.

## How Not To Relieve Financial Repression: Brazil in the Mid-1960s

If interest ceilings remain on both deposits and loans, only a very limited tilting of the banking system away from established "urban" channels toward higher-return "rural" investments is possible. On the one hand, small-scale loans are inherently high-cost and require rates far above customary ones or the existing legal maxima. On the other hand, the limited current deposit base of the banks in most LDCs makes significant lending to small enterprises impossible without an unacceptable contraction in funds available to large urban borrowers.

These points are well illustrated by Brazilian financial policy of recent years. Because of the relative neglect of agriculture in the 1950s—particularly in the impoverished Northeast—the government literally forced banks in the 1960s to expand agriculture's share in total bank credit relative to agriculture's contribution to gross national product. Superficially at least, this seems like an appropriate response to the underlying problem of financial repression, with which we have been so concerned. Moreover, agriculture in Brazil has been the victim of a highly discriminatory foreign trade policy as well.[13]

Unfortunately, these loans to agriculture were made at rates of interest well *below* the average rate of inflation. Indeed, the standard commercial lending rate seems to have been 24 percent (nominal) for commerce and manufacturing, with legislation passed in 1964 requiring that rural credit be extended at not more than three-fourths of the commercial rate, that is, 18 percent.[14] (Actually both of these nominal lending rates of interest were substantially lower prior to 1965, when the "standard" base rate was only 12 percent.) In contrast, the average rate of price inflation in Brazil from 1955 to 1967 seems to have been on the order of 35 to

13. See Nathaniel H. Leff, *Economic Policy-Making and Development in Brazil: 1947–1964* (John Wiley, 1968).

14. A complete analysis of the relative shares of credit going to agriculture and industry, relative rates of interest, and bank policy is to be found in Judith Tendler, "Agricultural Credit in Brazil" (U.S. Agency for International Development, October 1969; processed). The analysis in this section draws freely on this most interesting paper.

40 percent, as measured by the wholesale price index. (See Table 8-7.) Hence, the real return on holding money was highly negative. Moreover, the rate of inflation was too unstable (ranging from 13 to 91 percent) for the banks to offset it by appropriately adjusting nominal rates of interest on deposits or loans even if they could legally have done so.

As in many other Latin American countries, these negative real rates of interest charged by banks in Brazil were so far below market equilibrium that the allocation of the limited supply of organized credit was turned into a purely political struggle. In November 1970, Señor Edgard Perez, President of the Federation of Southern Brazilian Wheat Cooperatives, complained in a speech before the President of Brazil that the 18 percent nominal rate was excessively high for investments in grain storage facilities, "given the low return on such projects." He went on to urge that the Brazilian government immediately open a "special line of credit to the producers' cooperatives, specifically for the construction of silos and warehouses, at a zero interest rate if possible. . . ."[15] It should be noted that the marketing of wheat is completely controlled by the Bank of Brazil, and all wheat is sold at a high government-supported price. Subsidized credit in large quantities has been available from the Bank of Brazil for this activity, and even lower rates have been available for purchases of agricultural machinery, fertilizers, and soil correctives used in wheat production.[16]

Since the government felt obliged to "do something" for agriculture, it simply instructed the Bank of Brazil to provide agricultural credit directly and attempted to get the commercial banks to do the same. Needless to say, the lower agricultural lending rate —the inverse of the appropriate relationship in view of higher agricultural lending costs—caused most commercial banks to subvert this process as far as possible. The Bank of Brazil—less hampered by profit considerations—continued to provide most of the agricultural banking credit. Even so, there was a substantial relative shift of credit to agriculture in the 1960s in comparison to the 1950s, as Judith Tendler has calculated. (See Table 7-1.)

15. "Federação das Cooperativas Triticolas do R. G. Sul Apresenta Sugestoes ao Presidente Medici Para Auto-Suficiencia do Trigo," *Jornal do Brasil* (November 26, 1970). I am indebted to Peter T. Knight of the Ford Foundation for the translation.

16. Peter T. Knight, *Brazilian Agricultural Technology and Trade: A Study of Five Commodities* (Praeger, 1971), Chap. 4.

TABLE 7-1. *Credit Outstanding as a Percentage of Current Production in Brazilian Agriculture, Industry, and Commerce, 1955–66*

| Year | Agriculture | Industry and commerce |
|------|-------------|-----------------------|
| 1955 | 9.4  | 45.0 |
| 1956 | 8.9  | 44.0 |
| 1957 | 8.0  | 44.9 |
| 1958 | 9.5  | 46.4 |
| 1959 | 11.0 | 43.3 |
| 1960 | 10.4 | 44.5 |
| 1961 | 10.9 | 40.8 |
| 1962 | 10.1 | 39.9 |
| 1963 | 13.1 | 31.2 |
| 1964 | 10.7 | 29.5 |
| 1965 | 10.0 | 31.0 |
| 1966 | 13.9 | 26.4 |

Source: Judith Tendler, "Agricultural Credit in Brazil" (U.S. Agency for International Development, 1969; processed), Table 2.

Growth in value added was substantially higher in industrial than in agricultural production. Nevertheless, the real value (deflated by the wholesale price index) of outstanding bank credit to commerce and industry stayed about constant—despite this industrial growth. On the other hand, the real value of these credit balances outstanding to agriculture about doubled over the 1955–66 interval. The results—shown in Table 7-1—were a modest rise in the ratio of agricultural credit to output from a very low initial level, and a quite spectacular drop in the ratio of bank credit to production in industry and commerce.[17] The latter was due at least as much to the shrinkage in the real size of the banking system over this interval and the more intensive use by the government of bank credit as it was to the switch of credit from industry to agriculture. The negative real rates of interest paid by borrowers were, of course, passed on to depositors who, not surprisingly, reduced the real value of their deposits. This process of financial decline in Brazil is documented more fully in Chapter 8. (Later the decline was partially reversed beginning in 1968, after a

17. This squeeze on formal bank credit might have been offset slightly by the growth of "financeras," which were less hampered by formal interest-rate restrictions in discounting commercial paper and in issuing notes to small savers. Nevertheless, they were high-cost and quite unstable institutions.

"monetary correction" factor reflecting the actual rate of inflation was added to interest rates on certain classes of loans and deposits. For illustrative purposes, the analysis of Brazil in this book ends with the mid-1960s.)

It is very difficult to assess the net favorable impact on Brazilian agriculture of the increased availability of organized bank lending. Total bank credit still is very small in relation to total real output, in view of the dependence of farmers on informal credit markets. The lack of interest-rate rationing makes it difficult to tell whether the loans really were used for high-priority purposes. Indeed, the banks were given incentives not to lend to small farmers because of the fixed interest charge and because of allowances for administrative expenses, which, perversely, were actually higher for large loans benefiting established farmers and agricultural intermediaries. The net effect of the credit switch was probably to benefit agriculture slightly.

There is little doubt, however, of the importance of the contraction in the real supply of industrial credit in the Brazilian industrial stagnation of the mid-1960s:

> The perplexing thing about the Brazilian economic situation in the 1960s was the simultaneous presence of inflation and relative stagnation. Over the four years 1963–66, the annual industrial growth rate fell from the 9.8 percent of the previous decade to 3 percent. Yet prices more than quadrupled during the period despite a variety of antiinflationary measures. The economy had the worst of both worlds, inflation without growth.[18]

After examining a variety of explanations for the stagnation, Samuel Morley concluded that the remarkable contraction in the real volume of bank credit significantly reduced the supply capacity of Brazilian industry. It did so by restricting the amount of working capital available to Brazilian firms—the productive input most directly affected by the contraction in bank credit. Individual firms found it more expensive to hold inventories of finished goods, goods in process, and raw materials, and to extend trade credit to customers. There were actual shortages of key productive inputs that could not be financed economically from nonbank sources:

18. Samuel A. Morley, "Inflation and Stagnation in Brazil," *Economic Development and Cultural Change*, Vol. 19 (January 1971), p. 184.

But the crucial difference between the fully developed financial system of the United States and that of Brazil is that here no firm would ever have to forego expansion because of lack of credit to finance the required working capital. There are many nonbank sources of funds comparable in terms and cost, so that restrictive monetary policy would probably never affect supply. In Brazil, by contrast, banks are the principal source of funds. . . . While there has been a rapid development in recent years of nonbank financial intermediaries ["financeras"] selling so-called letters of exchange, their cost is high and they are available mostly to well-known firms.[19]

Paradoxically, there was one urban activity that did not decline during the inflation and financial squeeze of the mid-sixties. Excessive numbers of bank branches were opened in urban enclaves in Brazil to attract noninterest-bearing deposits of "convenience." The inflation had caused interest rates on deposits to fall relative to the more easily adjusted lending rates, both being negative in real terms. Without interest rate competition, the banks were induced to compete for customers by simply setting up branches in apartments or offices serving the well-to-do. But marble banking palaces or politicians on bank payrolls are *not* to be confused with an expansion in the real stock of money. A similar paradox has been described for Uruguay during a period of extraordinary inflation and financial decline:

> Uruguayan per capita GNP has been slowly declining (on the average) since about 1955; all sectors of the economy are beset with serious difficulties, and unemployment reached an estimated 12 percent in 1963. In the midst of this general decline, however, the banking sector has undergone a tremendous *physical* expansion. Between 1958 and 1964, the number of banks (counting branch offices) increased from 433 to 704—i.e., by 64 percent.[20]

## Orthodox Deflation and the Supply Constraint

The industrial recession in Brazil over the 1964–67 period was due as much or more to the reduction in the *real* size of the banking system (the money/GNP ratio declined to its historical nadir of 21 percent in 1966) as to the forced switch in the granting of credit from industry to agriculture. This contraction in the real stock of

19. *Ibid.*, pp. 197–98.
20. Herman E. Daly, "A Note on the Pathological Growth of the Uruguayan Banking Sector," *Economic Development and Cultural Change*, Vol. 16 (October 1967), p. 91.

money—and real bank credit—was due primarily to the extraordinary inflationary expectations built up in the early 1960s, when inflation accelerated from 54 percent in 1962 to 73 percent in 1963 to 91 percent in 1964. The real return to holders of money declined sharply. Thereafter, an "orthodox" policy of deflation was implemented, which slowed inflation to 51 percent in 1965, 37 percent in 1966, and 25 percent in 1967. It was during the latter period, however, when rates of inflation were declining, that the industrial recession bit most sharply.

A similar phenomenon has been observed in other countries. As is well known in Latin America, the orthodox deflationary measures recommended by the Klein-Saks mission to Chile were successful in dampening threatened hyperinflation in 1955, at the apparent expense of a severe industrial recession that lasted from 1956 to 1958.[21] The real stock of money in Chile also fell to an historical low of less than 10 percent of GNP in the 1955–58 period. (See Table 8-4, below.) The associated decline in output and employment was enough to give "orthodox" deflationary advice a bad reputation throughout all of Latin America.

Moreover, the emerging slump in the construction and some consumer goods industries and the resulting unemployment and discontent, particularly in Santiago, may have dampened the President's zeal for any vigorous prosecution of the stabilization program. The momentum of the program carried through to 1957 during which prices rose by only 17 per cent, but in 1958 the reins were definitely loosened and the rate of inflation returned to a lively 33 per cent. Throughout this period, moreover, the economy stagnated and per capita income actually declined. Chile seemed to have chosen for itself the worst of several possible worlds, since it had "neither stability nor development," to quote the title of a brochure by one of its most articulate economists.[22]

Is a contraction in real output the burden that must be borne in the short run in order to dampen high and unstable inflation over the long run? In fact, the answer is "no," and some rather striking counterexamples of successful price stabilization are provided in Chapter 8. But the brute fact remains that deflation has been associated with painful reductions in output and employment

21. For a discussion of the Klein-Saks mission, see Albert O. Hirschman, *Journeys Toward Progress: Studies of Economic Policy-Making in Latin America* (Twentieth Century Fund, 1963), pp. 199–217.
22. *Ibid.*, p. 211.

in many developed and less developed countries. The Chilean and Brazilian experiences are not isolated examples.

In avoiding an economic depression, the crucial difference between *successful* and *unsuccessful* price stabilization is the distinction between contraction in *nominal* as opposed to *real* monetary variables. In Chapter 4, above, it was suggested that the rate of change in the price level could be reduced if the central bank restricted the percentage rate of change in the nominal stock of money, as denoted by $\dot{M}$. Such a policy remains necessary in order to eliminate inflation. But $M/P$—the real stock of money—does not have to fall with the stock of money $M$ or $\dot{M}$. Quite the contrary. The real return on holding money, $d - \dot{P}^*$, can be made to rise quickly in the course of deflation by a credible fall in price movements expected in the future, coupled with a suitable and delicately adjusted rise in nominal rates of interest, $d$, paid to depositors. The two together can be sufficient to maintain the private demand to hold real money balances at a high level. Hence the syndrome of allowing real bank credit to contract while deflating, as experienced by Chile and Brazil, can be avoided.

The unorthodox idea of preserving or even augmenting the real stock of money in the course of a price stabilization program bears further examination. This need to maintain a large $M/P$ is not evident from the Keynesian theory of deflation, where the emphasis is simply on reducing aggregate demand or the inflationary gap by monetary and/or fiscal measures. Insofar as it emphasizes the need to reduce short-run aggregate demand in order to achieve price stabilization, the Keynesian model may be quite perverse in implying that a reduction in the real stock of money—and the corresponding real stock of bank credit on the other side of the balance sheet—is a welcome and necessary contribution to the deflation process. This unfortunate conclusion arises because the Keynesian model does not recognize that a contraction in the real stock of money reduces the aggregate supply of goods and services. That is, real cash balances—and the associated bank intermediation—are a vital input into productive processes in the short periods of time over which deflations occur.

In contrast to this Keynesian view, *complementarity* between the real stock of money and the stock of capital holds during short-run deflations as well as over longer periods of balanced growth. In the process of deflation over the short run, the key component of investment that is influenced most by monetary policy is working capital, as is demonstrated by Samuel Morley's analysis of the Brazilian deflation.[23] In moderately wealthy LDCs, such as Brazil and Chile, the real supply of bank credit to some manufacturing and commercial concerns has become large enough to be vital to their operation. (This is less true in a more primitive economy like Indonesia.) With plant capacity essentially fixed during the time period over which one hopes the deflation will occur, an incidental contraction in $M/P$ in the course of trying to control $\dot{M}$ may well force severe disintermediation on the banking system. This in turn forces firms dependent on bank finance to reduce working capital: inventories of goods in process, trade credit, and advances to workers prior to the actual sales.

The result is unemployed labor and underutilized plant capacity. For lack of financing for key inputs—replacement parts, various semi-finished materials, labor services—entire factories may be shut down. To draw an imperfect analogy, precipitously cutting off or reducing the supply of real bank credit constricts aggregate output much like cutting off the supply of electric power, water, or some other vital input.

Deflation of aggregate demand will be self-defeating if it creates bottlenecks in the aggregate supply of goods and services. After all, the price level will fall (or stop rising) only if the aggregate demand for goods and services is reduced relative to their aggregate supply. Hence any measure that accentuates "financial repression," by reducing the already limited efficiency of the bank-oriented capital markets, will be inordinately expensive. It may cause the aggregate supply of goods and services to fall faster than the fall in aggregate demand and thus frustrate attempts to stabilize the price level.

But there is an apparent dilemma. Price deflation requires monetary stringency in some form. Isn't the orthodox panoply of monetary controls—ceilings on nominal bank credit outstanding, increased reserve requirements, limited rediscount tranches, and so on—necessary to balance the aggregate demand and supply of nominal money at a noninflationary level? And if this "orthodox" advice is followed, won't restraint on the real volume of bank

23. Morley, "Inflation and Stagnation in Brazil."

lending be a necessary consequence? After all, the initial impact of these orthodox prescriptions is to force a banking contraction, which in turn may easily multiply in standard textbook fashion.

By themselves these orthodox direct restraints on the *supply* of money and credit are indeed likely to bring misery and hardship in their wake. One can, however, deflate in a quite different way. Instead of operating directly to reduce the supply of money and credit at disequilibrium rates of interest, the authorities can *increase the demand for money* by raising expected returns to the holders of money. During the initial inflation, real rates of interest are likely to become severely depressed to negative levels. When a serious (believable) attempt at deflation is undertaken, with $\dot{M}$ brought under control and nominal rates of interest on bank deposits raised sharply to be commensurate with remaining inflationary expectations, the demand for real money balances will increase. Correspondingly, there will be a reduction in the demand for commodities as individuals rush to acquire cash balances. Individually, firms and households will try to increase holdings of $M$, and, in the aggregate, the stock of $M/P$ in the economy will increase.

The desired deflationary impact on the aggregate demand for commodities will be achieved, thereby reducing the rate of increase in the price level, even as the competitiveness and real size of the banking system increases. Real credit—albeit at much higher nominal rates of interest—can then expand rather than contract, and the typical squeeze on working capital can be avoided altogether.

In short, aggravated financial repression is not a necessary consequence of price stabilization. The key is to deflate by means of increased real interest rates, which increase the demand for money, rather than to rely primarily on a credit contraction at low disequilibrium rates of interest that reduce the supply of money.

But it is not enough to point out conceptually how the prototype Brazilian and Chilean deflations were unnecessarily costly. One would like firm evidence that price stabilization without tears is feasible in less developed countries generally and that increases in real cash balances and physical investment are indeed complementary, as our theory would suggest. Such evidence is provided in Chapter 8.

# 8

# Monetary Reform and Successful Financial Growth

THIS CRITIQUE OF monetary policies in the less developed countries (LDCs) can be fully justified only if it is demonstrated that the financial repression commonly observed is *not* endemic. To be convincing, one needs to explain how repression comes about and to show that its release is well within the control capabilities of monetary and fiscal authorities in poor countries. We now turn to the latter, more pleasant task.

Our basic thesis of complementarity between money and capital implies that large and fast-growing real cash balances, $M/P$, contribute to rapid growth in investment and in aggregate output. Furthermore, for official policies to make a critical difference in the real size of the monetary system, the private sector must be quite sensitive to the real interest rates chosen for deposits and loans. Low, possibly negative, real lending and deposit interest rates shrink $M/P$. Correspondingly, measures taken to relieve such repression markedly expand $M/P$. Is there any statistical evidence of high correlation between $M/P$ and growth on the one hand, and the sensitivity of the public's responsiveness to changes in the real return on holding money on the other?

Among wealthy countries, Japan and Germany provide rather striking examples of sustained monetary growth relative to gross national product (GNP) even some years after recovery from the Second World War had taken place. These two countries illustrate what a fully developed monetary system might approximate in a rapidly growing economy, and they are analyzed in some detail below. But no country now classified as "less developed" has followed fully successful financial policies over the entire postwar period. Indeed, a few LDCs, such as Argentina, Brazil, and Chile, showed a financial decline compared to what they had achieved in earlier eras, although they were somewhat atypical in this respect. Most poor countries showed neither continual financial decline nor the spurt of financial growth necessary to break the repression syndrome.

There are, however, a few LDCs that suffered from all the consequences of financial repression for a number of years and then undertook a remarkable policy shift toward increased real deposit and lending rates that favorably altered the future course of their economies. Korea in 1964–66 and Indonesia in 1967–69 displayed turning points where real monetary expansion had an immediate buoyant impact on capital accumulation and output. Taiwan, on the other hand, did not display as "sharp" a reversal in financial strategy, but it has used high deposit and lending rates over a longer period of time to encourage successful financial growth. All three are currently in the financially "transformed" category, although their monetary systems have not yet grown to the same proportion of GNP as have those of Germany and Japan; nor is there any assurance that any of the three countries won't relapse back to more repressive policies. Yet all three are useful vehicles for completing our analysis of successful but "nonorthodox" programs for stabilizing the price level.

For organizational convenience, the analyses of financial growth in this chapter ignore the foreign sector and concentrate on domestic real rates of interest and money/GNP ratios—particularly the volatile performance of time and savings deposits. In practice, exchange-rate policy, international flows of capital, and trade restrictions have all been critical ingredients in the success or failure of past attempts at monetary reform. Hence, the interaction between the foreign sector and domestic financial policies is treated comprehensively in Chapter 11.

## Sustained Financial Growth: Germany and Japan from 1953 to 1970

Although Germany and Japan had major monetary reforms in 1948 and 1949, this study will focus on the longer-run pattern of financial growth after these interesting reforms occurred. One should remember that the Second World War devastated the banking systems of both countries. Inflation wiped out any large carry-over of assets and liabilities from the past and severely shook the public's confidence in holding money. In these two important respects, both monetary systems could be considered to have started *de novo* from the 1948–49 reforms, although each carried over a strong banking tradition from earlier eras.

Since wartime rebuilding had been largely completed by 1953, that year appears to be a reasonable base for gauging the pattern of sustained financial development in peacetime in two rapidly growing economies *after* the immediate changes associated with currency stabilization had occurred. Germany and Japan are particularly interesting because in both the banking system dominates the capital market and direct finance is less important than in other advanced countries. As we have seen, indirect finance via the banking system is also the dominant mode in developing countries.

Table 8-1 offers a statistical picture of growth of the Japanese money supply narrowly defined as $M_1$ (currency and demand deposits) and the more broadly defined $M_2$, which includes time and savings deposits as well. $M_1$ remains a fairly stable proportion of GNP, ranging from about 28 percent of GNP in 1953 to about 30 percent in 1970. However, time and savings deposits rise sharply from near equality (with currency plus demand deposits) in 1953 to being more than twice as great in 1970. This enormous relative growth in time and savings deposits is responsible for boosting $M_2$ from 57 percent of GNP in 1953 to about 98 percent in the late 1960s. The ratio of monetary liabilities to GNP—the mirror image of outstanding bank finance provided to both government and the private sector—seems to be the simplest measure of the importance or "real size" of the monetary system in the economy, and it is

TABLE 8-1. *The Financial Structure of Japan, 1953–70*
Monetary and GNP data in billions of current yen

| Year | Money supply | | | Gross national product | Ratio of $M_2$ to GNP | Whole-sale price index | Con-sumer price index |
| | Demand deposits plus currency ($M_1$) | Time and savings deposits | Total ($M_2$) | | | ($1953 = 100$) | |
|---|---|---|---|---|---|---|---|
| 1953 | 1,937 | 2,015 | 3,952 | 6,965 | 0.567 | 100 | 100 |
| 1954 | 2,013 | 2,543 | 4,556 | 7,792 | 0.585 | 99 | 105 |
| 1955 | 2,331 | 3,064 | 5,395 | 8,525 | 0.633 | 97 | 103 |
| 1956 | 2,714 | 3,837 | 6,551 | 9,508 | 0.689 | 102 | 104 |
| 1957 | 2,824 | 4,767 | 7,591 | 11,071 | 0.686 | 105 | 108 |
| 1958 | 3,185 | 5,870 | 9,055 | 11,342 | 0.798 | 98 | 109 |
| 1959 | 3,711 | 7,236 | 10,947 | 12,794 | 0.856 | 99 | 110 |
| 1960 | 4,420 | 8,937 | 13,357 | 15,214 | 0.878 | 100 | 114 |
| 1961 | 5,258 | 11,095 | 16,353 | 18,487 | 0.885 | 101 | 121 |
| 1962 | 5,725 | 13,360 | 19,085 | 21,999[a] | 0.868 | 99 | 128 |
| 1963 | 7,702 | 15,493 | 23,195 | 24,464 | 0.948 | 101 | 138 |
| 1964 | 8,704 | 17,996 | 26,700 | 28,838 | 0.926 | 101 | 143 |
| 1965 | 10,287 | 20,905[b] | 31,192 | 31,787 | 0.981 | 102 | 154 |
| 1966 | 11,716 | 24,601 | 36,317 | 36,545 | 0.994 | 106 | 162 |
| 1967 | 13,369 | 28,635 | 42,004 | 43,107 | 0.974 | 106 | 168 |
| 1968 | 15,155 | 33,548 | 48,703 | 51,148 | 0.952 | 107 | 177 |
| 1969 | 18,282 | 39,904 | 58,186 | 59,705 | 0.975 | 110 | 187 |
| 1970 | 21,358 | 47,038 | 68,396 | 70,580 | 0.969 | 114 | 201 |

Source: International Monetary Fund, *International Financial Statistics*, various issues.
a. Discontinuous data with a slight upward adjustment.
b. Change in data series with a slight downward adjustment in totals.

used throughout this chapter. By this measure the Japanese monetary system is particularly large, as is clear from the comparisons with other countries made later in this chapter.

The German experience, as portrayed in Table 8-2, is strikingly parallel to the Japanese. Time and savings deposits rose from about two-thirds of $M_1$ in 1953 to about two and one-half times $M_1$ in 1970. Throughout the period, $M_1$ remained stable as a proportion of GNP at about 16 or 17 percent, but $M_2$ increased from 29.7 percent of GNP in 1953 to 52 percent in 1970.

The rapidly rising $M_2$, however, is not a particularly comprehensive measure of the overall lending capacity of the German banking system because of the unusual German banking practice

TABLE 8-2. *The Financial Structure of Germany, 1953–70*
Monetary and GNP data in billions of current deutsche marks

| | Money supply ($M_2$) | | | Gross national product | Ratio of $M_2$ to GNP | Ratio of $M_2$ plus bank bonds to GNP | Wholesale price index | Consumer price index |
| Year | Demand deposits plus currency ($M_1$) | Time and savings deposits | Bank bonds | | | | ($1953 = 100$) | |
|---|---|---|---|---|---|---|---|---|
| 1953 | 23.4 | 16.5 | 6.0 | 134.3[a] | 0.297 | 0.342 | 100 | 100 |
| 1954 | 26.5 | 21.0 | 8.6 | 145.4[a] | 0.327 | 0.386 | 99 | 100 |
| 1955 | 29.2 | 25.3 | 10.6 | 180.4 | 0.302 | 0.361 | 100 | 102 |
| 1956 | 31.3 | 29.8 | 12.3 | 198.8 | 0.307 | 0.369 | 102 | 104 |
| 1957 | 35.1 | 37.0 | 13.1 | 216.3 | 0.333 | 0.394 | 103 | 107 |
| 1958 | 39.7 | 43.7 | 14.4 | 231.5 | 0.360 | 0.422 | 103 | 109 |
| 1959 | 44.4 | 52.6 | 17.2 | 250.9 | 0.387 | 0.455 | 102 | 110 |
| 1960 | 47.4 | 60.4 | 20.6 | 296.8 | 0.363 | 0.433 | 103 | 111 |
| 1961 | 54.5 | 67.3 | 24.4 | 326.2 | 0.373 | 0.448 | 105 | 114 |
| 1962 | 58.0 | 76.6 | 29.0 | 354.5 | 0.380 | 0.461 | 106 | 117 |
| 1963 | 62.2 | 88.6 | 34.3 | 377.6 | 0.399 | 0.490 | 106 | 121 |
| 1964 | 67.6 | 102.5 | 41.2 | 413.7 | 0.411 | 0.511 | 108 | 124 |
| 1965 | 72.7 | 119.8 | 47.7 | 460.4 | 0.418 | 0.522 | 110 | 128 |
| 1966 | 74.0 | 139.7 | 51.5 | 490.7 | 0.436 | 0.540 | 112 | 133 |
| 1967 | 81.5 | 161.6 | 53.5 | 494.6 | 0.492 | 0.600 | 111 | 134 |
| 1968 | 88.4 | 196.2 | 59.0 | 538.9 | 0.528 | 0.638 | 105[b] | 136 |
| 1969 | 93.6 | 223.4 | 66.3 | 602.8 | 0.526 | 0.636 | 107[b] | 140 |
| 1970 | 102.7 | 250.3 | 78.1 | 679.0 | 0.520 | 0.635 | 114[b] | 145 |

Source: Same as Table 8-1.
a. Downward-biased GNP series due to data discontinuity.
b. Discontinuity with value added tax excluded from calculations of wholesale price index.

of issuing long-term bonds as a substitute for deposits in attracting funds. The rising importance of these bond issues relative to demand deposits is indicated in the third column of Table 8-2. Let the sum of these bond issues and $M_2$ be taken as a measure of lending capacity (as distinct from the provision of liquidity services) and denote it by $M_3$. In measuring the flow of German bank financing, $M_3$ is comparable to $M_2$ by itself in the case of Japan and most LDCs. $M_3$ rose from being one-third of German GNP in 1953 to 63.5 percent of GNP in 1970. (The ratio of money to GNP in four other industrial countries is shown in Table 8-3.)

In contrast, the ratio of $M_2$ to GNP averaged about 25 percent in the late 1960s for the "typical" semiindustrial LDCs portrayed in Table 8-4—even though LDCs tend to be relatively more de-

TABLE 8-3.  *The Ratio of the Money Supply ($M_2$) to Gross National Product in Four Industrial Countries, 1950–70*

| Year | Belgium | France[a] | United Kingdom | United States |
|------|---------|-----------|----------------|---------------|
| 1950 | ... | 0.32 | ... | 0.65 |
| 1951 | ... | 0.31 | 0.66 | 0.60 |
| 1952 | ... | 0.30 | 0.63 | 0.62 |
| 1953 | 0.60 | 0.32 | 0.61 | 0.61 |
| 1954 | 0.59 | 0.34 | 0.61 | 0.65 |
| 1955 | 0.59 | 0.36 | 0.56 | 0.63 |
| 1956 | 0.57 | 0.36 | 0.54 | 0.62 |
| 1957 | 0.55 | 0.35 | 0.53 | 0.61 |
| 1958 | 0.59 | 0.33 | 0.53 | 0.66 |
| 1959 | 0.61 | 0.34 | 0.54 | 0.63 |
| 1960 | 0.60 | 0.47 | 0.52 | 0.63 |
| 1961 | 0.62 | 0.51 | 0.51 | 0.66 |
| 1962 | 0.62 | 0.52 | 0.51 | 0.67 |
| 1963 | 0.63 | 0.53 | 0.50 | 0.69 |
| 1964 | 0.60 | 0.53 | 0.50 | 0.70 |
| 1965 | 0.60 | 0.55 | 0.50 | 0.71 |
| 1966 | 0.61 | 0.56 | 0.51 | 0.68 |
| 1967 | 0.61 | 0.59 | 0.54 | 0.71 |
| 1968 | 0.63 | 0.60 | 0.55 | 0.70 |
| 1969 | 0.61 | 0.58 | 0.54 | 0.66 |
| 1970 | 0.59 | ... | 0.56 | 0.70 |

Source: Same as Table 8-1.
Note: Comparable ratios for Japan and Germany are given in column 5 of Tables 8-1 and 8-2.
a. Time and savings deposits are not included in 1950–59 data.

**TABLE 8-4.** *The Ratio of the Money Supply ($M_2$) to Gross National Product in Eleven Semiindustrial Less Developed Countries, 1950–69*

| Year | Argentina | Brazil | Chile | India[a] | Philippines | Turkey | Ceylon | Colombia | Pakistan | Peru | Venezuela |
|------|-----------|--------|-------|----------|-------------|--------|--------|----------|----------|------|-----------|
| 1950 | 0.52 | 0.38 | ... | 0.19 | 0.23 | 0.18 | 0.29 | 0.16 | ... | 0.20 | 0.16 |
| 1951 | 0.44 | 0.36 | ... | 0.17 | 0.20 | 0.18 | 0.28 | 0.17 | ... | 0.18 | 0.16 |
| 1952 | 0.42 | 0.36 | ... | 0.18 | 0.20 | 0.18 | 0.28 | 0.18 | ... | 0.20 | 0.17 |
| 1953 | 0.45 | 0.34 | ... | 0.17 | 0.20 | 0.20 | 0.26 | 0.19 | ... | 0.21 | 0.18 |
| 1954 | 0.48 | 0.32 | ... | 0.20 | 0.19 | 0.22 | 0.28 | 0.20 | ... | 0.20 | 0.18 |
| 1955 | 0.48 | 0.29 | 0.11 | 0.22 | 0.21 | 0.22 | 0.27 | 0.20 | ... | 0.21 | 0.19 |
| 1956 | 0.46 | 0.28 | 0.10 | 0.21 | 0.21 | 0.24 | 0.31 | 0.24 | ... | 0.22 | 0.21 |
| 1957 | 0.42 | 0.30 | 0.09 | 0.22 | 0.22 | 0.24 | 0.29 | 0.21 | ... | 0.22 | 0.25 |
| 1958 | 0.42 | 0.30 | 0.09 | 0.22 | 0.22 | 0.21 | 0.29 | 0.21 | ... | 0.21 | 0.26 |
| 1959 | 0.29 | 0.30 | 0.11 | 0.24 | 0.23 | 0.19 | 0.29 | 0.21 | ... | 0.21 | 0.25 |
| 1960 | 0.29 | 0.31 | 0.12 | 0.23 | 0.23 | 0.20 | 0.30 | 0.21 | 0.22 | 0.20 | 0.22 |
| 1961 | 0.28 | 0.32 | 0.13 | 0.23 | 0.26 | 0.21 | 0.31 | 0.23 | 0.19 | 0.21 | 0.22 |
| 1962 | 0.24 | 0.33 | 0.14 | 0.25 | 0.27 | 0.20 | 0.31 | 0.25 | 0.20 | 0.21 | 0.21 |
| 1963 | 0.26 | 0.30 | 0.12 | 0.24 | 0.28 | 0.20 | 0.33 | 0.23 | 0.22 | 0.23 | 0.21 |
| 1964 | 0.28 | 0.23 | 0.15[b] | 0.23 | 0.24 | 0.22 | 0.34 | 0.21 | 0.25 | 0.23 | 0.22 |
| 1965 | 0.24 | 0.26 | 0.16[b] | 0.25 | 0.24 | 0.24 | 0.34 | 0.22 | 0.25 | 0.22 | 0.23 |
| 1966 | 0.25 | 0.21 | 0.17[b] | 0.25 | 0.25 | 0.25 | 0.33 | 0.21 | 0.28 | 0.21 | 0.22 |
| 1967 | 0.27 | 0.23 | 0.17[b] | 0.22 | 0.27 | 0.26 | 0.33 | 0.22 | 0.24 | 0.20 | 0.23 |
| 1968 | 0.29 | 0.24 | 0.18[b] | 0.24 | 0.29 | 0.27 | 0.31 | 0.22 | 0.26 | ... | 0.24 |
| 1969 | 0.29 | 0.25 | 0.18[b] | 0.25 | 0.30 | 0.29 | 0.29 | 0.24 | ... | ... | ... |

Source: Same as Table 8-1.
a. Indian data are calculated on the assumption that measured national income is four-fifths of unmeasured GNP.
b. Upward shift in index due to a change in the GNP series.

pendent on their banks to provide finance external to investing enterprises. The German and Japanese banking systems are now *between two and five times as large* (measured by the ratio of their liabilities to GNP) as those in LDCs. These marked statistical differences in the real size of the monetary systems in the two sets of countries, combined with the earlier analysis of financial repression, are consistent with the banking-financial system's being a leading force in the rapid postwar growth of Japan and Germany.

Of course, causation is not necessarily unidirectional. Rapidly growing economies that have received their impetus to develop from other sources may generate an unusual growth in demand for financial assets, including money. The nexus between growth and the demand for financial assets is explored more fully in the theoretical model developed in Chapter 9. At the very least, however, it does seem that financial repression could well impede incipient growth—a point that will become clearer when the physiology of successful monetary reforms is investigated.

## The Choice of a Price Index for Measuring the Real Return on Money

What real return on holding money, a combination of expected inflation and weighted nominal deposit interest rates, did individuals and firms see in Germany and Japan in the 1953–70 period? Treating expected inflation first, there are two related issues: (1) what price index appropriately measures price-level movements for purposes of holding money; and (2) how are expectations about price movements in the future formed and related to actual movements in the chosen index? The choice of an appropriate price index is no small matter in economies where per capita productivity growth is very high and real wages are rising sharply. Typically, this productivity growth causes the price of services to rise vis-à-vis commodities, since the former are generally more labor-intensive and less subject to (measurable) technical innovations.[1] Therefore, the consumer price index (CPI), which

1. There is usually substantial statistical ambiguity in separating services outputs from measured inputs as, for example, in construction and medical activities. Thus technical change in the service industries is usually understated, with the result that measured price increases in indices with high service components may be "too great."

has a large service component, will rise faster than the wholesale price index (WPI), since the latter consists exclusively of commodities.

The Japanese case provides rather spectacular evidence of this divergence in price indices, as can be seen from the difference between the last two columns in Table 8-1. The WPI is essentially stable for the eleven years 1953–64 and then begins to rise slowly, although in 1970 it was still only 14 percent higher than it was in 1953. In contrast, the CPI rises quite rapidly over the whole period until in 1970 it is about double what it had been in 1953. The same qualitative divergence between the German CPI and WPI is apparent in the last two columns of Table 8-2, although the difference is somewhat less because German productivity growth has not been as great as that of the Japanese. Differences of this order of magnitude between the WPI and CPI do not seem to exist in the less developed countries, except for those few whose real wages have risen sharply.

It is presumed here that proportional changes in the WPI are appropriate measures of "the" $\dot{P}$ (defined as the proportional change in $P$, the chosen price index), which should enter as an important component of the real return on holding money. The basic reason is that tangible physical capital, that is, inventories of commodities of all kinds, is the principal alternative asset open to savers—which may be either substitutable or complementary with real money balances, as explained in Chapter 6. In other words, pure services cannot be "held" in asset portfolios and be subject to intertemporal reallocations of the kind described in the Fisherian model presented in Chapter 2. Even households that save with the ultimate intention of consuming services in the distant future must hold those savings in the form of either goods or financial assets. Hence, it is primarily the rate of change of *commodity* prices that wealth holders compare with nominal rates of interest on financial assets in deciding on their stocks of money and near-monies relative to their incomes and relative to their holdings of goods.

Once the decision is made to use $\dot{P}$ based on the WPI, then the interpretation of $\dot{P}^*$—expected price changes—becomes quite simple for Japan and Germany over the 1953–70 interval. The WPI was remarkably stable throughout the period, although a little inflation concentrated in the later 1960s may have some influence on price expectations in the 1970s. Hence, financial development over the period can reasonably be considered to have taken place under stable prices and expectations of continuing price stability. This is, of course, quite consistent with the enormous real financial growth that actually did take place.

This price stability implies that nominal rates of interest on deposits, plus the convenience of using banking facilities and hand-to-hand currency, by themselves approximate "the" real rate of return seen by German and Japanese holders of money. While the convenience yield cannot be estimated quantitatively, banking facilities are widespread throughout the urban and rural areas of both countries; and "the" nominal return on holding money must be treated as the weighted average of interest rates on various kinds of deposits and noninterest-bearing currency.

In the case of Japan, time deposits of three months bear a rate of interest of 4 percent, which rises to 5.75 percent on one-year time deposits.[2] (The rate was 5.5 percent until April 1970.) These rates seem to have been stable over most of the 1953–70 period because they were legal maxima. In Germany the rate on one-year time deposits has been close to 5 or 5.5 percent over most of the period, but it had risen to nearly 7 percent at the end,[3] possibly reflecting increased inflationary pressure. Interest rates on bank bonds were typically a percentage point or so higher. These "real" rates were evidently high enough to attract the extraordinary flow of time and savings deposits actually observed.

## Monetary Growth, Self-Finance, and Intersectoral Flows of Saving

A description of the German and Japanese experiences should include some brief comment on sources of saving, sectoral financial surpluses, and structural change associated with real financial growth. From Goldsmith's data, it is known that the less developed countries remain heavily dependent on self-finance and that relatively little household saving is tapped by "organized" business

2. Office of the Prime Minister, Bureau of Statistics, *Japan Statistical Year Book,* 1970 (Japan Statistical Association, 1971), p. 358, and relevant preceding issues.

3. *Monthly Report of the Deutsche Bundesbank* (Frankfurt), relevant issues.

activities.[4] Indeed, this is the major reason why their capital markets remain fragmented with widely dispersed rates of return. In contrast, the personal sector in Japan has consistently provided about 50 to 55 percent of total net saving in the economy since the early 1950s, whereas corporate business has provided only about 20 percent—government saving being responsible for the remainder. However, corporate business generally undertook more than 50 percent of new investments—mostly from the large financial surplus transferred from the personal sector through the banking system.[5] About two-thirds of net investment of nonfinancial corporations—above the relatively small capital consumption allowances—were financed in this way. Hence, Japanese corporations were heavy users of external funds, and their reliance on self-finance was quite limited.

While it is common knowledge that Japanese personal saving remained unusually high throughout the period, a more remarkable shift in sources of savings occurred in Germany, where the household share of the economy's aggregate net saving rose from 23 percent over the period 1950–54 to 54 percent in the years 1965–68. There was a corresponding relative decline in the business share of net saving from 41 percent in the period 1950–54 to 14 percent from 1965 through 1968.[6] The aggregate propensity to save remained high and stable during this marked shift in the sources of net saving. Ray interpreted this phenomenon as part of a general decline in subsidized self-financed investment—which was dominant immediately after the German monetary reform in 1949—and the current more prevalent use of unsubsidized finance "external" to the user enterprise.[7] Indeed, in both Germany and Japan, business firms are major holders of time and savings deposits, which are, of course, sources of finance for other corporate borrowers.

In wealthy economies, which are more financially mature than Germany and Japan because their financial systems did not have

4. See Chapter 4, note 1.
5. See Jiro Yao, "Supply of Funds and Currency for Economic Growth," in Jiro Yao (ed.), *Monetary Factors in Japanese Economic Growth* (Japan: Kobe University, 1970), pp. 27–59.
6. Data taken from Edward J. Ray, "Finance in a Development Context: Lessons from West Germany" (Ph.D. thesis, Stanford University, 1971), which in turn were compiled from various issues of the Deutsche Bundesbank *Monthly Report*.
7. "Finance in a Development Context."

to be completely rebuilt in the later 1940s, one expects much less pronounced changes in sources of net saving. Indeed, internally financed investment within large established enterprises is more common in Britain and in the United States. In the developing countries, on the other hand, great economic transformation is necessary. Hence, one would expect that "economic development" —reducing the dispersion in rates of return on various assets— would require inter- and intrasectoral transfers of the same extraordinary magnitudes as those experienced by Germany and Japan. A large banking sector seems quite capable of accomplishing this with a high level of efficiency through the voluntary actions of firms and households. Unfortunately, the more usual method in LDCs is to maintain a small and repressed monetary system and then to rely on a battery of fiscal and other interventions in commodity and factor markets as a substitute for bank intermediation. The unhappy consequences of these various second-best devices for allocating capital were explored in Chapter 3.

## *Notes on Financial Decline in Argentina, Brazil, and Chile*

The unsatisfactory attempts at "orthodox" deflation in Brazil and Chile described in Chapter 7 were, in part, responses to a real financial decline that had been taking place over a more prolonged period of time, a decline that is also visible in Argentina. This decline was associated with inflation and the cumulative buildup of inflationary expectations into the early 1960s from what these same countries had experienced in the twenties and thirties. Knowledge of these particular economies is useful, not because they are representative of what happens in most LDCs with no history of a more golden financial age, but because the three illustrate the sensitivity of the real size of the banking system to a monetary policy that is at the opposite end of the spectrum from that chosen by Germany and Japan.[8]

The financial data on Argentina, Brazil, and Chile are again

8. One should again note that financial policy in both Brazil and Argentina changed in the later 1960s and early 1970s toward growth, although it is still too early to tell whether or not this change will be sustained.

drawn from the published statistics of the International Monetary Fund on $M_2$, GNP, and the wholesale and consumer price indices. Unfortunately, the IMF's data tabulation begins only with 1950, and even then there are significant gaps in the Chilean data for the early 1950s. Nevertheless, the three countries' $M_2$/GNP ratios of the 1960s are roughly of the same magnitude as those of the melange of less developed countries, which were tabulated in Table 8-4.

John Deaver has traced the Chilean real stock of money from the late 1920s to its nadir in the mid-1950s.[9] Despite the fact that price inflation was significant at about a 7 percent rate prior to 1932, it began to accelerate, averaging 20 percent over the years 1932–55, and reached a maximum of about 80 percent in 1955. The rate of inflation has fluctuated in an unstable fashion around an average of 35 percent since then. Data in the Deaver study indicate that the $M_2$/GNP ratio fell in 1955 to about two-fifths of what it had been in 1931–32. As one can see from Table 8-5, the ratio has remained remarkably small, fluctuating between 9 percent and 18 percent of GNP since then.

Similarly, Adolfo Diz[10] has traced the marked decline in the real size of the Argentinian $M_2$/GNP ratio from 46 percent in 1935 to its nadir of about 24 percent in 1962. During this period, he calculated that the rate of price inflation fluctuated around an average of about 16 percent, being significantly higher in the later 1950s and early 1960s. The inflation was maintained at the 16 to 20 percent level in the later 1960s, when the ratio $M_2$/GNP recovered slightly from its low point. (See Table 8-6.) As in the case of Chile, the size of the Argentinian financial sector remains small and restricted, whether one compares it to fast-growing economies like those of Germany and Japan or with its own past experience.

Brazil had a noticeable decline in the $M_2$/GNP ratio, from 38 percent in 1950 to about 21 percent in 1966, associated with high and unstable inflation. (See Table 8-7.) The consequent repressive impact on Brazilian capital markets was analyzed in Chap-

9. John V. Deaver, "The Chilean Inflation and the Demand for Money," in David Meiselman (ed.), *Varieties of Monetary Experience* (University of Chicago Press, 1970).

10. Adolfo Cesar Diz, "Money and Prices in Argentina, 1935–1962," in Meiselman (ed.), *Varieties of Monetary Experience*.

TABLE 8-5. *The Financial Structure of Chile, 1950–70*
Monetary and GNP data in undeflated millions of pesos

| Year | Money supply | | | Gross national product | Ratio of $M_2$ to GNP | Whole-sale price index | Con-sumer price index |
| | Demand deposits plus currency ($M_1$) | Time and savings deposits | Total ($M_2$) | | | (1963 = 100) | |
|---|---|---|---|---|---|---|---|
| 1950 | ... | ... | ... | 153 | ... | 3 | 2 |
| 1951 | ... | ... | ... | 186 | ... | 4 | 3 |
| 1952 | ... | ... | ... | 260 | ... | 4 | 4 |
| 1953 | ... | ... | ... | 350 | ... | 6 | 5 |
| 1954 | ... | ... | ... | 586 | ... | 9 | 8 |
| 1955 | 93 | 16 | 109 | 1,026 | 0.11 | 16 | 15 |
| 1956 | 130 | 25 | 155 | 1,633 | 0.10 | 25 | 23 |
| 1957 | 165 | 38 | 203 | 2,274 | 0.09 | 33 | 29 |
| 1958 | 222 | 54 | 276 | 2,959 | 0.09 | 41 | 36 |
| 1959 | 294 | 162 | 456 | 4,145 | 0.11 | 57 | 51 |
| 1960 | 384 | 211 | 595 | 4,895 | 0.12 | 62 | 57 |
| 1961 | 432 | 265 | 697 | 5,457 | 0.13 | 62 | 61 |
| 1962 | 556 | 389 | 945 | 6,595 | 0.14 | 68 | 69 |
| 1963 | 747 | 459 | 1,206 | 9,827 | 0.12 | 100 | 100 |
| 1964 | 1,129 | 720 | 1,849 | 12,493[a] | 0.15 | 152 | 146 |
| 1965 | 1,867 | 997 | 2,864 | 17,547[a] | 0.16 | 202 | 188 |
| 1966 | 2,594 | 1,524 | 4,118 | 24,312[a] | 0.17 | 256 | 231 |
| 1967 | 3,241 | 2,149 | 5,390 | 31,814[a] | 0.17 | 306 | 273 |
| 1968 | 4,481 | 3,219 | 7,700 | 42,882[a] | 0.18 | 391 | 345 |
| 1969 | 6,068 | 4,910 | 10,978 | 61,437[a] | 0.18 | 532 | 451 |
| 1970 | 10,051 | 6,563 | 16,614 | ... | ... | 727 | 598 |

Source: Same as Table 8-1.
a. Downward shift in GNP data series.

ter 7. As in the case of Chile and of Argentina, one would not have to go very far back into the history of this century to find a relatively larger and healthier Brazilian financial sector. The state of repressed finance cannot be taken as necessary or "indigenous" to Latin America in particular or to underdeveloped economies in general.

## Sensitivity of Time and Savings Deposits

One further aspect of the rise and decline of the financial sector deserves attention. From the above analysis of the German and Japanese economies, it becomes quite clear that holdings of in-

TABLE 8-6. *The Financial Structure of Argentina, 1950–70*
Monetary and GNP data in undeflated billions of pesos

| Year | Money supply | | | Gross national product | Ratio of $M_2$ to GNP | Whole-sale price index | Con-sumer price index |
| | Demand deposits plus currency ($M_1$) | Time and savings deposits | Total ($M_2$) | | | | |
| | | | | | | ($1963 = 100$) | |
|---|---|---|---|---|---|---|---|
| 1950 | 25 | 11 | 35 | 68 | 0.52 | ... | 5 |
| 1951 | 30 | 11 | 42 | 95 | 0.44 | ... | 6 |
| 1952 | 34 | 12 | 47 | 112 | 0.42 | ... | 9 |
| 1953 | 43 | 15 | 58 | 129 | 0.45 | ... | 9 |
| 1954 | 52 | 18 | 70 | 145 | 0.48 | ... | 10 |
| 1955 | 61 | 20 | 81 | 171 | 0.48 | ... | 11 |
| 1956 | 71 | 29 | 100 | 217 | 0.46 | 12.4 | 12 |
| 1957 | 83 | 30 | 113 | 271 | 0.42 | 15.5 | 16 |
| 1958 | 119 | 41 | 160 | 385 | 0.42 | 20.4 | 20 |
| 1959 | 170 | 46 | 216 | 737 | 0.29 | 47.5 | 44 |
| 1960 | 218 | 62 | 280 | 956 | 0.29 | 54.8 | 55 |
| 1961 | 243 | 77 | 320 | 1,140 | 0.28 | 59.5 | 63 |
| 1962 | 250 | 90 | 340 | 1,403 | 0.24 | 77.6 | 80 |
| 1963 | 322 | 131 | 453 | 1,725 | 0.26 | 100.0 | 100 |
| 1964 | 459 | 191 | 650 | 2,360 | 0.28 | 126.1 | 122 |
| 1965 | 592 | 263 | 855 | 3,604 | 0.24 | 156.3 | 157 |
| 1966 | 787 | 337 | 1,124 | 4,490 | 0.25 | 187.5 | 207 |
| 1967 | 1,092 | 465 | 1,557 | 5,871 | 0.27 | 235.3 | 268 |
| 1968 | 1,364 | 642 | 2,006 | 6,832 | 0.29 | 258.9 | 311 |
| 1969 | 1,508 | 795 | 2,303 | 7,982 | 0.29 | 273.7 | 335 |
| 1970 | 1,796 | 995 | 2,791 | ... | ... | 312.3 | 380 |

Source: Same as Table 8-1. Ratios and totals are calulated from data before rounding.

terest-bearing time and savings deposits were really much more volatile over sustained periods of time than is money narrowly defined, that is, currency and demand deposits. Indeed, time and savings deposits rose from being about equal to $M_1$ in 1953 to being about two and one-half times as great as $M_1$ in 1970 in these two countries.

The converse was true during the large negative changes in the inflation-prone Latin American economies. John Deaver's data can be used to show that, in the period of financial decline in Chile, the ratio of time and savings deposits to $M_1$ fell from about 186 percent in 1928 to about 12 percent in 1955. Similarly, in the case of the Argentinian decline, Adolfo Diz calculated that the same

TABLE 8-7.  *The Financial Structure of Brazil, 1950–70*
Monetary and GNP data in undeflated millions of cruzeiras

| | Money supply | | | | | Whole- | Con- |
| | Demand deposits plus currency | Time and savings | Total | Gross national | Ratio of $M_2$ to | sale price index | sumer price index |
| Year | ($M_1$) | deposits | ($M_2$) | product | GNP | ($1963 = 100$) | |
|---|---|---|---|---|---|---|---|
| 1950 | 78 | 19 | 97 | 252 | 0.38 | 4 | 4 |
| 1951 | 91 | 20 | 111 | 305 | 0.36 | 5 | 4 |
| 1952 | 104 | 21 | 125 | 351 | 0.36 | 6 | 5 |
| 1953 | 124 | 22 | 146 | 427 | 0.34 | 7 | 6 |
| 1954 | 151 | 25 | 176 | 554 | 0.32 | 9 | 7 |
| 1955 | 178 | 24 | 202 | 689 | 0.29 | 10 | 9 |
| 1956 | 217 | 25 | 242 | 880 | 0.28 | 12 | 11 |
| 1957 | 291 | 29 | 320 | 1,053 | 0.30 | 13 | 13 |
| 1958 | 353 | 33 | 386 | 1,304 | 0.30 | 15 | 15 |
| 1959 | 501 | 39 | 540 | 1,791 | 0.30 | 21 | 20 |
| 1960 | 692 | 57 | 749 | 2,397 | 0.31 | 27 | 27 |
| 1961 | 1,042 | 67 | 1,109 | 3,475 | 0.32 | 38 | 37 |
| 1962 | 1,702 | 71 | 1,773 | 5,436 | 0.33 | 58 | 57 |
| 1963 | 2,792 | 106 | 2,898 | 9,520 | 0.30 | 100 | 100 |
| 1964 | 5,191 | 172 | 5,363 | 22,904[a] | 0.23 | 191 | 187 |
| 1965 | 9,104 | 265 | 9,369 | 36,424[a] | 0.26 | 289 | 303 |
| 1966 | 10,470 | 769 | 11,239 | 53,216[a] | 0.21 | 396 | 444 |
| 1967 | 14,931 | 1,389 | 16,320 | 70,699[a] | 0.23 | 496 | 575 |
| 1968 | 21,460 | 2,727 | 24,187 | 98,957[a] | 0.24 | 615 | 714 |
| 1969 | 28,670 | 3,914 | 32,584 | 131,883[a] | 0.25 | 739 | 880 |
| 1970 | 35,920 | 4,993 | 40,913 | ... | ... | 902 | 1,048 |

Source: Same as Table 8-1.
a. Upward shift in GNP data series.

ratio fell from about 136 percent in 1935 to about 29 percent in 1962 (based on a slightly different data series than the IMF uses). During the peak of the Brazilian inflation in 1963–65, savings and time deposits dwindled to less than 4 percent of the money supply narrowly defined.

Of course, what happens to the ratio of time and savings deposits to $M_1$ depends on the nominal interest rate on deposits, and not just on the rate of inflation. Indeed, by being willing to pay a nominal interest rate greater than 20 percent on some classes of time deposits in the 1960s, Chile was able to restore time and savings deposits to about five-sixths of $M_1$ by 1969—even though the overall size of the banking system remained unduly small.

It seems broadly true, therefore, that periods of great financial growth are associated with price stability and a disproportionately rapid increase in the growth of time and savings deposits. Conversely, periods of inflation and financial decline are associated with disproportionate shrinkage in these less liquid time and savings deposits. Because time and savings deposits are not directly usable as a means of payment in the very short run, they are more adversely affected by a high average rate of inflation or great instability in the rate of inflation. High and unstable inflation is difficult to offset with a correspondingly high and variable nominal interest rate on some classes of deposits, both because of administrative practicality and because the anticipated real return is unstable in the minds of potential holders of money.

Yet, high interest rates on savings and time deposits may be used to offset moderate inflation—as will be seen in the cases of Korea and Taiwan—and remain extremely valuable devices for indicating the true scarcity of capital to potential savers. Currency and demand deposits are less useful for this purpose, because of the greater administrative difficulty in paying a nominal interest rate to money holders or, alternatively, continuously reducing the aggregate price level in order to increase the real return on money. Hence, time and savings deposits remain the key—if volatile— element in achieving the real growth in the banking system necessary to relieve financial repression.

## Financial Reform without Tears: Korea, 1964–70

We have examined financial growth and decline over fairly long periods of time, amounting to fifteen years or more. In most LDCs, however, the time horizon of both politicians and economists is considerably shorter than this. Any major change in strategy—say, away from inflation and toward financial growth—must be accompanied by the assurance of an immediate increase in real income, or at least no significant decline, in order to be accepted by policymakers. Hence, it is of the greatest importance to extend our theoretical schema, supported by empirical evidence, to demonstrate that a carefully chosen set of techniques for deflating can have an immediate payoff. Fortunately the Korean experience after 1964 is an ideal vehicle for such a demonstration.

The deflation of 1955–58 in Chile and the similar contraction of 1964–67 in Brazil were both characterized by severe bank disintermediation, which imposed an unusual squeeze on the availability of working capital in addition to the "normal" financial distortions to which firms had become accustomed. Disintermediation resulted from the buildup of inflationary expectations that reduced the real return on holding money, and from an "orthodox" deflationary policy in the form of credit ceilings, reduced rediscount tranches, increased reserve requirements, and so on, that contributed further to a contraction. The resulting restraint on the aggregate supply of goods and services was all too apparent from the analysis in Chapter 7.

These unfortunate episodes suggest an alternative and less orthodox approach to achieving price stabilization. Instead of directly restricting bank lending, measures can be taken to increase directly the demand to hold real money balances, $M/P$. A significant rise in nominal bank deposit and lending rates would be sufficient to raise the corresponding real rates rather sharply, if the government's control over the rate of expansion in nominal cash balances, $\dot{M}$, also dampened inflationary expectations. Price inflation would be ended as individuals switched from commodities to money. Stocks of commodities used as hedges against inflation would be dishoarded. Instead of bank disintermediation, however, real bank lending would expand. A rapid rise in bank intermediation—although at much higher rates of interest—would relieve supply bottlenecks, associated in part with the scarcity of working capital, which had been plaguing the economy for some time. Investment of higher productivity than the prevailing average would increase as entrepreneurs embarked on a number of highly profitable ventures because of their newly found access to bank finance. Aggregate output in the economy would surge forward without the customary pause that has come to be associated with deflationary policies, because financial repression would be reduced rather than accentuated.

In essence, this nonorthodox or "intermediation-led" model of price stabilization was successfully followed by the Koreans in

1965; and it neatly illustrates the basic complementarity between $M/P$ and capital accumulation in the short run, as well as over more extended periods of time.

For almost a decade after the end of the Korean war in 1954, development in that country followed a sporadic but typical LDC growth pattern, with some successes and some retrogressions, but showed no clear indication of a major breakout from a low-level income trap. Virtually all of its imports were financed by U.S. aid transfers or military counterpart funds during this decade. The absence of sustained growth, despite heavy aid transfers from abroad, caused South Korea to be unfavorably compared (in the late fifties and early sixties) to North Korea by many commentators. Disequilibrium interest rates on both loans and deposits prevailed in the organized banking system so that a traditional curb market of small moneylenders was the principal, but limited, source of finance external to Korean business enterprise. There was an ebb and flow to inflation, with some variation in the real size of the organized banking system around a level that remained small in real terms. However, inflation did accelerate in 1963 and 1964 (see Table 8-8) and presented the government with a rather acute control problem.

Two major reforms occurred during the 1964–65 interval in the areas of foreign trade and of policy toward public and private savings.[11] The change in foreign trade policy included a devaluation and unification of the multiple system of exchange rates, which was completed by the spring of 1965. There was a simultaneous increase in public saving through increased tax collections and increased user charges on outputs of government-owned industries, such as utilities. These reduced the government's dependence on the issue of fiat money as a source of revenue and were vital in bringing $\dot{M}$ under more conscious policy control—although this control was not complete because of some foreign exchange complications that will be treated in Chapter 11.

In addition, in September 1965, there was a major banking re-

11. The fascinating details of these reforms are discussed by Gilbert T. Brown in U.S. Agency for International Development, "Economic Policy and Development: A Case Study of Korea in the 1960's" (AID, March 1971; processed), and by S. Kanesa-Thasan, "Stabilizing an Economy—A Study of the Republic of Korea," International Monetary Fund, *Staff Papers*, Vol. 16 (March 1969), pp. 1–26.

form that raised the official ceiling on nominal interest rates on time and savings deposits from 15 to 30 percent, with some scaling down of rates on time deposits of shorter maturities.[12] The weighted average return on all classes of time and savings deposits was maintained at very high levels, about 24 percent (nominal) in 1966, with some slight reduction thereafter as inflation lessened. This financial reform was aimed at both increasing private savings and drawing private capital from the curb markets into the "organized" financial system.[13]

The rise in the real return on holding money depends on the rise in nominal interest rates and the expected decline in the rate of inflation. Column 9 in Table 8-8 shows the difference between the *maximum* nominal deposit rate on long-term time deposits and the *actual* rate of inflation. Hence it must be carefully qualified as a measure of the overall real return on money. The rate of inflation (column 7) may be a better measure (appropriately adjusted with a negative sign) of the real return on demand and shorter-term time deposits as well as currency. Either column, however, does show a remarkable increase in the real return on holding money, because the rate of inflation fell from an average of about 19.5 percent a year in 1960–64 to 8 percent a year during 1965–69 and augmented the effect of the sharp rise in nominal interest rates. *Hence, the net increase in the real return ranged from about 11 percentage points on demand deposits to about 26 percentage points on time deposits of the longest maturity.*

The resulting increase in the size of the Korean banking system was quite spectacular. The $M_2$/GNP ratio rose from its nadir of about 9 percent in 1964 to reach approximately 33 percent by 1969. Because of the accompanying spurt in investment, output, and employment, the increase in the *real* money stock was even greater. In 1969, $M_2$/WPI was *seven* times what it had been in 1964! As in the case of Germany and Japan, time and savings de-

---

12. A table with the complete structure of bank deposit and lending rates in Korea appears in Anand G. Chandavarkar, "Some Aspects of Interest Rate Policies in Less Developed Economies: The Experience of Selected Asian Countries," International Monetary Fund, *Staff Papers*, Vol. 18 (March 1971), p. 91.

13. The impetus for this remarkable reform arose out of a recommendation by John G. Gurley, Hugh T. Patrick, and E. S. Shaw in "The Financial Structure of Korea" (United States Operations Mission to Korea, July 1965; processed). I am deeply indebted to E. S. Shaw for many subsequent conversations on the Korean experience.

TABLE 8-8. *The Financial Structure of Korea, 1960–70*
Monetary and GNP data in billions of current won

| | Money supply | | | | | Whole-sale price index (1963 = 100) (6) | Percentage change in WPI (7) | Interest rate on one-year time deposits[b] (percent) (8) | Real return on holding one-year time deposits[c] (percent) (9) | Ratio of M₂ to WPI (10) |
| Year | Demand deposits plus currency (M₁) (1) | Time and savings deposits[a] (2) | Total (M₂) (3) | Gross national product (4) | Ratio of M₂ to GNP (5) | | | | | |
|---|---|---|---|---|---|---|---|---|---|---|
| 1960 | 22.1 | 5.9 | 28.0 | 246.7 | 0.1135 | 67 | ... | 10.0 | ... | 0.4179 |
| 1961 | 32.5 | 8.9 | 41.4 | 296.8 | 0.1395 | 76 | +13.4 | 12.1 | −1.2 | 0.5447 |
| 1962 | 35.1 | 16.6 | 51.7 | 348.6 | 0.1483 | 83 | +9.2 | 15.0 | +5.3 | 0.6229 |
| 1963 | 37.6 | 17.5 | 55.1 | 488.0 | 0.1129 | 100 | +20.5 | 15.0 | −4.6 | 0.5510 |
| 1964 | 48.9 | 14.7 | 63.6 | 696.8 | 0.0913 | 135 | +34.6 | 15.0 | −14.6 | 0.4725 |
| 1965 | 65.6 | 31.5 | 97.1 | 805.8 | 0.1205 | 148 | +9.9 | 18.8 | +8.1 | 0.6565 |
| 1966 | 85.2 | 70.2 | 155.4 | 1,032.0 | 0.1506 | 161 | +8.9 | 30.0 | +19.4 | 0.9646 |
| 1967 | 122.0 | 130.8 | 252.8 | 1,242.4 | 0.2035 | 172 | +6.5 | 30.0 | +22.1 | 1.4741 |
| 1968 | 153.6 | 255.5 | 409.1 | 1,575.7 | 0.2596 | 185 | +8.0 | 27.6 | +18.1 | 2.2078 |
| 1969 | 218.2 | 452.5 | 670.7 | 2,047.1 | 0.3276 | 198 | +6.7 | 24.0 | +16.2 | 3.3908 |
| 1970 | 305.6 | 585.2 | 890.8 | 2,545.9 | 0.3499 | 216 | +9.1 | 22.8 | +12.6 | 4.1279 |

Source: Same as Table 8-1. Percentages in column 7 and ratios in column 10 are calculated from unrounded data.

a. Excludes deposits with the Korean Reconstruction Bank.

b. Official ceilings on rates of interest. (Since these ceilings were subject to change within a calendar year, rough averages over the entire calendar year are presented in the table.) See Bank of Korea, *Monthly Economic Statistics*, Vol. 25, No. 11 (1971), p. 46.

c. $\dfrac{1 + (\text{col. 8})_t}{(\text{col. 6})_t \big/ (\text{col. 6})_{t-1}}$, where $t$ is the relevant year and $t − 1$ is the preceding year.

posits rose considerably more rapidly than demand deposits and currency—although the latter two also rose relative to GNP.

On the bank lending side, the reduced rate of inflation was accompanied by an increase in the standard (nominal) interest rate charged for bank loans from 14 to 26 percent a year—although about one-third of the total loans extended (such as those to exporters) were pegged in lower categories. Despite the sharp increase in the standard lending rate and the reduction in the rate of inflation, there was no shortage of private borrowers. The scarcity return on competitive investments seemed to be much higher than anyone had preconceived.

This book will not go into detail regarding techniques that the central bank might use to control the commercial banks, such as reserve requirements, special deposit accounts, rediscounting, and so on. So far, we have simply examined the impact of the banking system as a whole on nonbank holders of money and on borrowers. However, it seems worthwhile noting that, in November 1965, the Korean central bank raised its discount rate sharply from 10.5 to 21 percent and then relaxed its ceilings on the amounts commercial banks could discount at the new rate and also relaxed other specifications on the uses to which the discounted funds could be put.[14] This contrasts with the "orthodox" practice in deflations of tightening up with quantitative restriction on rediscounting and increased reserve requirements, but changing the discount rate (as well as other interest rates) relatively little.

Of course, the state of the government budget is a key variable in preventing expansion in nominal money above the growth in the public's demand to hold real balances; and the Korean government was successful in increasing tax revenue relative to expenditures in the 1964–66 period.[15] Because of the increased government saving, the rise in the real value of bank loans to the private sector was fully commensurate with the huge expansion of deposits.

The rise in output and employment growing out of the increase in investment and exports began right after the reforms took hold, so that the economy did not suffer temporary losses from the price stabilization program. Real output rose by 90 percent from 1965

14. Chandavarkar, "Some Aspects of Interest Rate Policies," p. 90.

15. One should note that the undeveloped state of the primary securities market in poor countries means that substantial government debt financing with the nonbanking public is not possible.

to 1969, whereas it had risen only 40 percent from 1960 to 1964 prior to the reforms. The average annual rate of inflation fell from about 19.5 percent over the four years preceding the reform to 8 percent afterward. Apparently the relaxation of the financial constraint on aggregate supply was enough to overcome any dampening influence on output from reduced aggregate demand. Unfortunately, it is the latter effect that is emphasized in traditional Keynesian *or* monetarist theories of short-run adjustment. These conventional theories associate a reduction in price inflation with a depression in aggregate output and employment because supply considerations, which are influenced by the state of the capital market, are outside their purview.

In summary, the banking system's role as an intermediary within the Korean economy expanded rather dramatically. The use of higher real rates of interest had the effect of sharply increasing household saving and drawing more existing capital through organized financial processes. The dependence of firms on self-finance and the traditional curb market was reduced correspondingly. In more general terms, the initial successful reduction in $\dot{M}$ by fiscal measures, together with the rise in nominal deposit interest rates promulgated by the central bank, were sufficient to reduce $\dot{P}$ while expanding $M/P$. From our theoretical analysis, one would expect a rise in the quality and quantity of investment—which indeed seems to have been the case, judging from the marked overall increase in Korea's real output and international competitiveness.[16]

## Monetary Growth in Indonesia with Constraints on Bank Lending

Detailed information of the kind available in Korea does not exist for Indonesia because of the subsistence nature of the economy and its more disorganized state prior to 1965. In particular, there are no really reliable indicators of aggregate real output, GNP, saving,

16. The large devaluation of the Korean *won* on the foreign exchange markets in 1964–65 was a necessary condition for Korean exports to grow. However, without a revival in investment and saving, exports could not have risen so spectacularly from 55 million U.S. dollars in 1962 to $622 million in 1969. (IMF, *International Monetary Statistics*, Vol. 23 [January 1970], p. 192, and Vol. 25 [February 1972]), p. 222.

or structural changes that may have occurred. Nevertheless, the International Monetary Fund's *International Financial Statistics* has recently collated enough monetary information for the 1965–70 period to demonstrate the short-run sensitivity of real cash balances to the real return on money, as presented in Table 8-9.

Since currency and demand deposits are still much greater than time and savings deposits and only modest rates of interest are paid on them, the real return on holding money in Indonesia is not very different from the rate of inflation, suitably adjusted with a negative sign. From Table 8-9 one can see the extremely high rate of inflation during the period 1965–67, which decelerated between 1968 and 1970. Correspondingly, our crude index of the *real* stock of money, $M_2$, divided by the Djakarta consumer price index, doubled by 1970 from its low point in 1967. Accompanying the financial reforms in 1968 was a major increase in interest rates paid on time deposits of one year maturity to 6 percent a month—which was subsequently reduced to 2 percent a month in 1970, as inflation decelerated. The increased real rate on time and savings deposits was a factor in their proportionately more rapid growth.

On the lending side, the financial system became completely dominated by state banks controlled by the Bank of Indonesia. Unlike the case of Korea, this bureaucratic structure may not have

TABLE 8-9. *The Financial Structure of Indonesia, 1965–70*
Monetary and GNP data in billions of current rupiahs

| Year | Money supply | | | Gross national product[a] | Ratio of $M_2$ to GNP | Consumer price index[b] (September 1966 = 100) | Ratio of $M_2$ to CPI |
|---|---|---|---|---|---|---|---|
| | Demand deposits plus currency ($M_1$) | Time and savings deposits | Total ($M_2$) | | | | |
| 1964 | ... | ... | ... | 7.0 | ... | 2 | ... |
| 1965 | 2.57 | 0.08 | 2.65 | 23.5 | 0.113 | 7 | 0.379 |
| 1966 | 22.21 | 0.34 | 22.55 | 311.0 | 0.073 | 76 | 0.297 |
| 1967 | 51.83 | 2.38 | 54.21 | 838.2 | 0.065 | 206 | 0.263 |
| 1968 | 113.20 | 12.50 | 125.70 | 1,973.9 | 0.064 | 470 | 0.267 |
| 1969 | 179.02 | 51.61 | 230.63 | ... | ... | 545 | 0.423 |
| 1970 | 241.06 | 80.01 | 321.07 | ... | ... | 612 | 0.525 |

Source: Same as Table 8-1.
a. Not a particularly reliable statistical series.
b. A consumer price index from the Djakarta area; wholesale prices are not available.

been capable of making efficient use of the sharp increase in additional resources (real deposits).

It [the Bank of Indonesia] largely controls the activities of the State banks; the latter are very much dependent on the Central Bank in regard to types and amounts of loans made, and very little initiative in almost any area comes from State banks. Bureaucratic red tape is profuse within this government structure—e.g., a potential borrower might have to wait for several months for word on his loan application. The State banks have little experience in making loans outside of the state-enterprise.[17]

If the banking system is not capable of directing its newly increased lending power into high productivity investments, then considerable social loss occurs both in the short run and over longer periods of time. Moreover, the immediate "frictional" costs of deflation will be greater if the banks do not have high-return loans available to offset the contraction in inventory investment (inflation hedges) as real money balances become more attractive. The trade-off between price stabilization and output growth will not be as favorable; and, unlike the immediate take-off in Korea, there was a significant lag in Indonesia before visible economic growth took hold after the monetary reform.

Priming the pump of economic development after years of stagnation is proving a slow and difficult business. But there has been progress in recent months. Earlier talk of recession has stopped. Budgetary development expenditure, though still lagging, has picked up substantially. Bank credit expansion has proceeded apace. While there is doubt whether much of this has gone to finance investment in fixed capital, a considerable number of infrastructure and industrial investment projects are making headway.[18]

Nevertheless, the consensus among observers seems to be that real output in Indonesia did not decline and probably rose during this period of sharp deflation with increased real deposit and lending rates. The allocation of resources seems to have been significantly improved, and monetization has been extended. Indonesian deposit holders appear to be highly sensitive to real rates of return, even if inputs were *not* appropriately applied to the intermediation process, as they were in Korea.

17. John G. Gurley, "Notes on the Indonesian Financial System" (paper prepared for delivery at the Dubrovnik Conference of the Development Advisory Service, Harvard University, June 1970; processed).

18. H. W. Arndt, "Survey of Recent Developments," *Bulletin of Indonesian Economic Studies,* Vol. 5 (November 1969), p. 1.

## *Receding Inflation and Declining Interest Rates in Taiwan*

The Korean and Indonesian experiences are particularly valuable in illustrating the economics of price stabilization with a sharp reversal from low to high real financial growth. Taiwan, on the other hand, is less useful for this purpose because in the ultimately successful stabilization program it undertook in the 1950s there were a few false starts and retrogressions. However, the Taiwanese banking system pioneered the introduction of very high deposit and lending rates during the 1950s—when the government's control over $M$ was still less than firm. These high rates were enough to offset cyclical inflation patterns, so that the $M_2$/GNP ratio rose from about 11 percent in the early 1950s to about 20 percent by the end of that decade. (See Table 8-10.)

The break-out to a pattern of financial growth significantly greater than that commonly observed in semiindustrial less developed countries became readily apparent only in the 1960s, when stability in the Taiwanese wholesale price index was achieved. The $M_2$/GNP ratio increased to 47 percent by 1970—which is very high by LDC standards, as may be seen from Table 8-4. Because of the accompanying remarkable growth in real GNP (per capita real income virtually doubled between 1960 and 1970), one should also note that the $M_2$/WPI ratio increased sevenfold. That is, the "real" lending capacity of the organized banking sector had risen almost seven times by 1970 from the more or less "normal" LDC level of financial development that had been achieved in 1960.

Somewhat surprisingly perhaps, *nominal* deposit and lending rates of interest *fell* during the rapid financial growth of the 1960s. The interest rate on one-year time deposits was reduced from 17.04 percent in 1960 to 9.72 percent in 1970. Deposits of shorter maturities—say one month—were kept lower and fell commensurately. The "standard" interest rate on secured loans—to which a complex of other loan rates are related—fell from 18 percent in 1960 to 12.6 percent by 1970.

But this fall in nominal rates need not be indicative of a fall in real rates. The measured "real" rate of interest during the 1960s

**TABLE 8-10. The Financial Structure of the Republic of China (Taiwan), 1950-70**

Monetary and GNP data in undeflated billions of new Taiwan dollars

| Year | Money supply Demand deposits plus currency (M₁) (1) | Money supply Time and savings deposits[a] (2) | Total (M₂) (3) | Gross national product (4) | Ratio of M₂ to GNP (5) | Wholesale price index (1963 = 100) (6) | Percentage change in WPI (7) | Interest rate on deposits[b] (percent) (8) | Real return on holding deposits[b] (percent) (9) | Ratio of M₂ to WPI (10) |
|---|---|---|---|---|---|---|---|---|---|---|
| 1950 | 0.58 | ... | 0.58 | ... | ... | 22.4 | ... | ... | ... | 0.026 |
| 1951 | 0.94 | ... | 0.94 | 10.82 | 0.0869 | 36.4 | +62.50 | ... | ... | 0.026 |
| 1952 | 1.29 | 0.52 | 1.81 | 15.75 | 0.1149 | 44.8 | +23.08 | ... | ... | 0.040 |
| 1953 | 1.68 | 0.69 | 2.37 | 21.20 | 0.1118 | 49.0 | +9.38 | 24.00 | 13.37 | 0.048 |
| 1954 | 2.13 | 0.88 | 3.01 | 23.15 | 0.1300 | 50.3 | +2.65 | 19.20 | 16.12 | 0.060 |
| 1955 | 2.56 | 1.03 | 3.59 | 27.88 | 0.1288 | 57.3 | +13.92 | 19.20 | 4.63 | 0.063 |
| 1956 | 3.23 | 1.07 | 4.30 | 32.30 | 0.1331 | 64.3 | +12.22 | 21.60 | 8.36 | 0.067 |
| 1957 | 3.80 | 2.18 | 5.98 | 37.99 | 0.1574 | 69.2 | +7.62 | 19.80 | 11.32 | 0.086 |
| 1958 | 5.13 | 3.82 | 8.95 | 44.44 | 0.2014 | 69.9 | +1.01 | 19.80 | 18.60 | 0.128 |
| 1959 | 5.57 | 4.99 | 10.56 | 51.73 | 0.2041 | 77.6 | +11.02 | 17.04 | 5.42 | 0.136 |
| 1960 | 6.11 | 6.25 | 12.36 | 62.56 | 0.1976 | 88.1 | +13.53 | 17.04 | 3.09 | 0.140 |
| 1961 | 7.34 | 10.24 | 17.58 | 69.79 | 0.2519 | 91.6 | +3.97 | 14.40 | 10.03 | 0.192 |
| 1962 | 7.92 | 13.01 | 20.93 | 76.47 | 0.2737 | 94.4 | +3.06 | 13.32 | 9.96 | 0.222 |
| 1963 | 10.20 | 17.18 | 27.38 | 87.34 | 0.3135 | 100.0 | +5.93 | 12.00 | 5.73 | 0.274 |
| 1964 | 13.43 | 21.73 | 35.16 | 102.21 | 0.3440 | 102.5 | +2.50 | 10.80 | 8.10 | 0.343 |
| 1965 | 14.84 | 25.50 | 40.34 | 112.87 | 0.3574 | 97.7 | -4.68 | 10.80 | 16.24 | 0.413 |
| 1966 | 17.39 | 32.32 | 49.71 | 125.55 | 0.3959 | 99.2 | +1.54 | 10.08 | 8.41 | 0.501 |
| 1967 | 22.10 | 38.92 | 61.02 | 143.04 | 0.4266 | 101.6 | +2.42 | 9.72 | 7.13 | 0.601 |
| 1968 | 24.89 | 43.54 | 68.43 | 167.98 | 0.4074 | 103.6 | +1.97 | 9.72 | 7.60 | 0.661 |
| 1969 | 28.92 | 53.07 | 81.99 | 190.81 | 0.4297 | 103.3 | -0.29 | 9.72 | 10.04 | 0.794 |
| 1970 | 35.09 | 66.50 | 101.59 | 217.64 | 0.4668 | 106.2 | +2.81 | 9.72 | 6.72 | 0.957 |

Sources: Deposit interest rate data, Anand G. Chandavarkar, "Some Aspects of Interest Rate Policies in Less Developed Economies: The Experience of Selected Asian Countries," IMF, *Staff Papers*, Vol. 18 (March 1971), p. 83; other data, International Monetary Fund, *International Financial Statistics*, various issues; and *The Republic of China, Taiwan Financial Statistics Monthly* (May 1971), published by Central Bank of China, Economic Research Department.

a. Includes lines 35 (quasi-money) and 45 (time and savings deposits) in *International Financial Statistics*.

b. Rate on one-year deposits.

c. See Table 8-8, note c.

on a one-year time deposit averaged more than 8 percent. (See column 9 in Table 8-10.) Given the high inflationary expectations established in the 1950s, the *expected* real rate probably rose in the minds of depositors as the decade of the 1960s progressed and inflation was curbed. This rise would certainly hold for currency, noninterest-bearing demand deposits, and low-interest time deposits of the shortest maturity, for which price stability is more important. Such a dampening of inflationary expectations is consistent with the extraordinary financial growth actually observed and with the measured private saving rate, which rose from 5 percent of GNP in 1960 to close to 12 or 13 percent by the end of the decade.[19]

## Summary

Putting all three of these LDC success stories together, what has been learned from them?

• It is within the monetary and fiscal capabilities of the developing countries to use high nominal rates of interest and control over $\dot{M}$ to embark on sharp changes in monetary policy away from repression and toward real financial growth.

• Stabilization of the price level need not be accompanied by an economic depression if policy permits the banking system to play its intermediary role.

• High nominal rates of interest can be juggled effectively to offset expected and experienced inflation if the latter is progressively reduced to "moderate" levels. It seems likely, however, that complete elimination of inflation in the wholesale price index is the preferred strategy.[20]

• Optimal *real* rates of interest on deposits and loans, for which capital-scarce economies should strive, are surprisingly high.

But be it remembered that:

• Financial repression is not very far away if monetary policy goes astray.

19. Chandavarkar, "Aspects of Interest Rate Policies," p. 83.

20. The argument here will be somewhat strengthened when foreign exchange considerations are introduced in Chapter 11.

# 9

## Optimum Monetization and Equilibrium Growth

THE POLICY IMPLICATIONS of financial repression (Chapter 7), and financial growth (Chapter 8) are evident. Some readers may find, however, that a theoretical overview of optimum monetary policy is helpful if only to distinguish the financial approach to capital accumulation used here from the neoclassical model with its full-liquidity optimization rule.[1] Imperfect capital markets imply that financial mechanisms are costly in their own use of labor and capital. What then are the marginal conditions to be satisfied, including the role of government seigniorage, when the monetary system is expanded to its optimum real size over a "long" time horizon?

The interaction between saving and growth also calls for a more explicit theoretical formulation. Monetary reform can stimulate growth in real output by raising saving propensities and the quality of capital formation. This point has been established and is not belabored further. But the reverse effect has not been emphasized heretofore: the buoyant impact of a high rate of growth in a progressive economy on the propensity to save and to acquire monetary assets. The closing of this virtuous circle is now portrayed within a modified version of a Harrod-Domar growth model; and then it is linked to a hypothetical shift from a state of

1. Milton Friedman, *The Optimum Quantity of Money and Other Essays* (Aldine, 1969). See also the analysis of the neoclassical full-liquidity rule in Chapter 5, above.

financial repression to one where "optimum" monetary policy is successfully employed.

Readers with a limited background in traditional monetary and growth theory can skip this chapter with little loss in continuity. Many important policy questions concerning international trade and capital movements remain for succeeding chapters. Here, the assumption of a closed economy is maintained, where government control over the rate of expansion in nominal cash balances, $\dot{M}$, the nominal interest rate on deposits, $d$, and ultimately the endogenous variable $M/P$, the real stock of money, are subject only to domestic influences.

## *The Optimum Supply of Monetary Services*

Monetary systems can be simple, or they can be bureaucratically complex. The banks themselves may use little real resources other than for the printing of notes, or they may be quite costly in using capital and skilled labor for managing loan portfolios or an extensive system of check clearing. The monetary authority may delegate lending decisions to profit-making commercial banks, while the central bank simply controls the total deposit liabilities of the commercial banks. Alternatively, the central bank may choose to retain the right to collect deposits directly and use its ability to issue coin and currency to undertake direct lending to the government or to other primary investors—since currency issue is the principal component of the money supply in more primitive economies. In practice, some combination of the two regimes is likely, but the absorption of resources by the banking system as a whole can still be systematically related to $M/P$. In order to construct a manageable model, however, some rather drastic analytical simplifications are necessary.

Assume that the banking system absorbs capital and labor "efficiently." It selects a combination of services to depositors of all classes (including holders of currency) such that the attractiveness of holding money of all forms is maximized for any given flow of real resources into the printing of notes, check clearing, and the servicing of time and savings deposits on the left-hand side of the balance sheet, and into the servicing of loan portfolios on the right-hand side. This assumption would rule out an overexpansion of the banks' physical plant, as occurred in the Brazilian and Uruguayan cases, noted in Chapter 7; and it would also rule out the type of inefficiency found in Indonesia (see Chapter 8), where the large banking bureaucracy failed to use newly gained deposits to seek out high-yield loans. In short, although net seigniorage or an inflation tax is extracted from the holders of money by the government, none of it is wasted through the banks' own misuse of resources.[2]

The second strong assumption involves the government's extraction of "seigniorage" or an inflation tax on real money balances through its ability to issue nominal money in return for goods and services. At one extreme, the government may maintain, at negligible cost in real resources, a very simple monetary system with no intermediation (lending) services provided to the private sector. In such a simple system, the proceeds from new money issue either go into government coffers or go to the holders of money through the interest paid on deposits.[3]

Instead, let us assume here that the government's appropriation of seigniorage is balanced against the social alternative of providing loan financing for the private sector at the *highest* rates of return that are realizable by the banking system. Other than the government's seigniorage, there are no favored borrowers receiving low-interest loans or other subsidies. The more seigniorage the government siphons off, the less is lent to the private sector, and consequently the earnings passed back to depositors are diminished. Depositors then respond by reducing their holdings of money. Thus, each equilibrium $M/P$ will have its own unique combination of government seigniorage and lending to the private sector that, over the long run, determine the real return to the holders of money—currency as well as deposits.

2. A more extensive analysis of this micro-allocation problem among deposit classes and currency is provided by Harry G. Johnson in "Problems of Efficiency in Monetary Management," *Journal of Political Economy*, Vol. 76 (September/October 1968), pp. 971–90.

3. This is essentially the assumption used in the voluminous neoclassical literature on the inflation tax. See, for example, Milton Friedman, "Government Revenue from Inflation," *Journal of Political Economy*, Vol. 79 (July/August 1971), pp. 846–56. The absence of bank intermediation is consistent with the existence of a perfect capital market in the private sector—a presumption that vitiates the whole neoclassical approach to less developed countries.

These assumptions regarding efficiency and seigniorage are very strong, but they do allow $M/P$ to be aggregated and then related to the real return on money, to the administrative costs of banking, and to the returns on new investments. These relationships are sketched in Figure 9-1, under the simplifying assumption that the level of income is given, an assumption that is relaxed later on.

As $M/P$ increases along the horizontal axis in Figure 9-1, there is an implicit change from a rather simple banking system issuing mainly coin and currency, where the government siphons off most of the seigniorage, to a more costly structure with a variety of deposit and loan classes. Bank intermediation within the private or quasi-public sectors becomes increasingly important, with most of the proceeds being channeled back to depositors. The curve $CD$ reflects those combinations of $M/P$ and the real return on holding money, $d - \dot{P}^*$ (where $\dot{P}^*$ is the expected future rate of inflation), which are on the "efficient" expansion path for the banking system as a whole. Each real return on $CD$ is consistent with the private

FIGURE 9-1. *The Optimum Supply of Monetary Services at a Given Income Level*

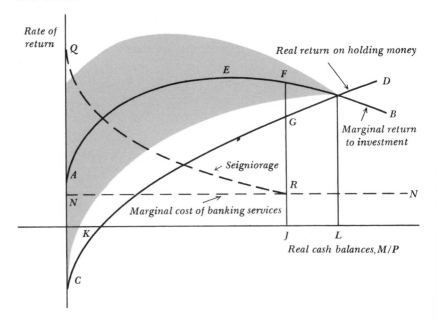

demand to hold the corresponding real money balances at the given level of income.

The social costs of expanding $M/P$ in this way are not negligible. Bankers eat and drink and must be housed—although not in a marble palace—at their place of work. The broken line $NN$ in Figure 9-1 is the marginal cost of servicing $M/P$ on the efficient expansion path measured as a percentage of $M/P$ itself. This cost is drawn to be a constant proportion of $M/P$ because of two offsetting considerations: the banking system gets more complex as its real size increases, and there are economies of scale in servicing larger numbers of depositors and borrowers. The net effect on marginal costs could go either way, and this important question is not analyzed further. The main point is that the social costs of increasing $M/P$ efficiently are substantial in a fragmented world, whereas the neoclassical model assumes such costs to be negligible.

Similarly, the shape of the dashed line $QR$ reflects government seigniorage, which, as a percentage of $M/P$, is high when real balances are small. The progressively reduced "cut" by the government is what permits the real stock of money to expand along the efficient expansion path described above. In Figure 9-1, seigniorage is measured as the vertical distance *above* $NN$, extending up to $QR$. The locus $QR$ itself then includes the real costs of maintaining the banking system, as well as the seigniorage being extracted by the government.

Finally, how can the rather strange looking curve $AB$ be interpreted as the marginal efficiency of investment in a world where rates of return are highly dispersed? It must be an average of all marginal investments undertaken at any specified $M/P$ for the economy as a whole, although some of these investments will appear intramarginal to individual entrepreneurs. Since bank intermediation increases with the real stock of money, the segment $AE$ of the curve $AB$ is one where the overall marginal return to investment in the economy actually *rises* along with investment itself. As the monetary system grows, "indivisibilities" in investment are overcome so that real returns actually increase over some significant range of new capital formation. This same injection of real inputs into the banking process reduces dispersion in earned rates of return to investment, as is shown by the progressively reduced shaded area around $AB$.

Once the rather cumbersome geometric machinery of Figure 9-1 is set up, the optimization rule becomes obvious. The banking system should be expanded until the real return on holding money, plus the marginal costs of providing banking services, are equal to the marginal return on new investments. This financial nirvana holds at point *J*, where *RJ* equals *GF*, and which I call the point of *optimum monetization*. Notice that dispersion in rates of return to investment is reduced, but not eliminated, at this optimum because of the cost of providing monetary services. Indeed, although the banking system is very large at point *J*, nonbank sources of finance—debt, equity, trade credit, insurance, and so on—thrive because of their access to specialized information or particularly convenient collateral. The presence of these nonbank financial sources reflects the unavoidable residual fragmentation in the capital market after optimum monetization is achieved.[4]

Most less developed countries fail to attain optimum monetization and remain repressed far to the left of point *J*, as was described in Chapter 7. But we also know from Chapter 8 that monetary reform—say, moving from *K* to *J* in Figure 9-1—is not only possible but highly desirable. Assuming that the efficient monetary expansion path, *CD*, is attained,[5] then government policy toward seigniorage becomes a crucial policy variable in expanding $M/P$ when reforms are undertaken. To reach optimum monetization, the government adjusts fiscal policy so that the extraction of seigniorage, shown to be zero at the optimum point *J*, is unnecessary. Thus, the monetary authorities are free to choose the preferred

---

4. In contrast, Friedman's full-liquidity optimizing rule requires further monetary expansion to the point *L*, where dispersion is eliminated altogether. Besides requiring heavy government subsidy to the banks, the point *L* is probably unattainable in any economically meaningful sense. In order that the marginal return on investment be identically equal to the real return on money, there must be no unsatisfied borrowers willing to sell securities at an expected rate of return greater than the return on money. Hence, under the full-liquidity rule, the monetary system would cannibalize all nonbank sources of finance! Bankers would become among the more numerous of the citizenry. This implausible implication of the concept of full liquidity has been suggested by S. C. Tsiang in "A Critical Note on the Optimum Supply of Money," *Journal of Money, Credit and Banking*, Vol. 1 (May 1969), pp. 266–80, in a slightly different context and is not pursued further here.

5. Lending to the private sector takes place at equilibrium rates of interest, and the banking bureaucracy operates efficiently—very strong assumptions indeed!

combination of $\dot{M}$ and $d$ that returns all the net earnings on bank portfolios to depositors, who respond by maintaining an appropriately large volume of deposits. Only then is there full financial liberalization in the sense that savers and investors "see" the correct rates of return.

The nature of the fiscal policy needed to support optimum monetization has been left implicit. But if the fiscal capacity of the government is unduly limited by, say, poor tax administration, then the temptation to divert seigniorage to the public exchequer, and indeed the social gain from doing so, will seem high. In a growing economy, such fiscal inadequacy can and often does take the form of tax revenue that is inelastic to income growth and government expenditures that are highly elastic. Hence, impulses to grow often result in budgetary deficits that are covered by appropriating seigniorage from the monetary system through currency issue or by forcing the banks to buy low-yield government securities. (Heavy sales of government securities to the nonbank public are simply not feasible in imperfect primary-security markets.) Such fiscal weakness aggravates financial repression by reducing the real return on holding money and may dampen the impulse to grow. Thus rather comprehensive fiscal reforms, examined in more detail in Chapter 10, are often necessary to sustain financial liberalization.

## Growth and Saving: The Virtuous Circle

*Economist:* Why do the Japanese save so much?
*Man on a Tokyo street:* Because our income grows so fast.

The propensity to save out of aggregate income is not a particularly useful parameter for analyzing repressed economies because rates of return on saving vary so widely. Unless one assumes that this dispersion in rates of return is given, new investment will have an indeterminate effect on aggregate output. However, once efficient monetary growth gets under way, this favorite parameter of all economists, from Marxists to neoclassicists, becomes worthy of closer examination.

The uncomfortable propensity of traditional theories to treat the propensity to save—albeit out of a given class of income—as a fixed parameter has been noted in Chapter 5. Moreover, much theory and even a few facts have been presented in Chapters 6 to 8 to suggest that saving rises as the attractiveness of money and near monies increases. Now let us concentrate on showing how *growth itself* increases the propensity to save out of aggregate income— the more so when holdings of real money balances are substantial.

The basic idea is simple enough. Given the "convenience" yield on liquid monetary assets (including time and savings deposits), firms and households typically maintain portfolio balance by keeping stocks of these assets in a certain balanced relationship with current income flows. Stocks of monetary assets will be high relative to income if the real return on holding money is high. Now suppose that the economy starts from a stationary state in which there is no net saving. Then economic innovation is introduced—say a "green revolution" or a monetary reform, or both. Aggregate income begins to grow and, because of economic interdependence, spreads its dividends to most households—even those that weren't directly affected by the initial innovation. But these households have portfolio targets for monetary (and other) assets relative to their fortuitously increased incomes. Thus, to maintain the ratio of money to income, they are induced to save—that is, they are induced *not* to consume all of their incremental income because they want their asset position to rise commensurately. Their propensity to save out of income is thereby increased.

This "portfolio effect" of growth on saving will be the more pronounced the higher is the desired ratio of money to gross national product (GNP) and, of course, the higher is the rate of growth. Individuals then find that they must save more, simply to maintain their money/income ratio. The effect on saving would be accentuated if there were stocks of physical assets (consumer durables, for example) that also rose with income. Japan and Taiwan would clearly qualify as being major beneficiaries of saving induced by the portfolio effect, but all nations are subject to it in greater or lesser degree. Indeed, it is the vein that governments tap when they appropriate seigniorage through the issue of nominal money in a growing economy. But such appropriation simply diverts the flow of private saving that an efficient banking system would otherwise convert into high-yield investments.[6] An optimal monetary strategy is one that weighs increased private investment against public seigniorage in determining how best to utilize the portfolio effect, and it seems worthwhile to incorporate growth more explicitly than was done in the purely static analysis of optimum monetization presented above.

A useful vehicle for illustrating the portfolio effect is a modified version of the venerable Harrod-Domar[7] model of equilibrium growth. In its original form, this model made no reference to financial considerations and assumed that saving was automatically transmitted into investment at a uniform rate of return. Hence the output/capital ratio—denoted by $\sigma$—was constant and yielded the simple production function:

$$(9\text{-}1) \qquad\qquad Y = \sigma K,$$

where $Y$ is aggregate real output (income) and $K$ is the stock of physical capital.

Implicitly, equation 9-1 assumes that technical change is sufficiently "labor augmenting" that the labor force need not enter explicitly as a separate constraint on production. Within our financial approach to economic development, the output/capital ratio could actually rise when new investment is accompanied by suitable monetary expansion; or investment could be subject to diminishing returns in the classical sense. For analytical simplicity, however, equation 9-1 will be used here, with $\sigma$ assumed to be constant.

The saving (investment) propensity in the unmodified Harrod-Domar model is simply a fixed proportion of income, denoted by $s$. That is,

$$(9\text{-}2) \qquad\qquad I = dK/dt = sY,$$

where $t$ is an index of time.

6. The neoclassical model does *not* close this circle, because real money balances are not viewed as a conduit for financing the accumulation of physical capital. Rather $M/P$ is treated as an independent form of wealth-holding by the private sector that acts as a *substitute* for the accumulation of physical capital—as shown in the analysis in Chapter 5. Thus the potentially favorable portfolio effect cannot easily be derived from established theory.

7. Evsey D. Domar, *Essays in the Theory of Economic Growth* (Oxford University Press, 1957); and Roy F. Harrod, *Towards a Dynamic Economics: Some Recent Developments of Economic Theory and Their Application to Policy* (London: Macmillan, 1948).

The equilibrium *percentage* rate of income growth, $\dot{Y}$, is obtained by substituting equation 9-1 into equation 9-2 to get

$$(9\text{-}3) \qquad\qquad \dot{Y} = \sigma s.$$

Equation 9-3 yields the familiar result that the rate of growth is the product of the marginal output/capital ratio and the marginal propensity to save. This condition for equilibrium growth continues to hold in the later analysis, even when the assumption of a fixed marginal propensity to save is modified.

Because of the portfolio effect of growth on saving, suppose now that the propensity to save is variable and is a function of the rate of growth, as is incorporated into equation 9-4 below. Saving is also influenced by a number of interacting variables—such as the real return on holding money—which determine the willingness of individuals to hold financial and other assets in a "convenient" ratio to their current income. Let the parameter $\rho$, given exogenously to the Harrod-Domar model, represent these "other" variables in the function describing the propensity to save:

$$(9\text{-}4) \qquad\qquad s = s(\dot{Y}; \rho),$$

where $0 < s < 1$; $\partial s / \partial \dot{Y} > 0$; and $\partial s / \partial \rho > 0$.

Equations 9-3 and 9-4 together define the equilibrium growth path for this variable-saving version of the Harrod-Domar model, once $\rho$ is given exogenously. That is, $\dot{Y}$ is defined by the implicit equation

$$(9\text{-}5) \qquad\qquad \dot{Y} = \sigma \cdot s(\dot{Y}; \rho).$$

The quantity $\dot{Y}$ now depends on the portfolio effect of *growth itself* operating on intended saving. The solution to equation 9-5 is portrayed graphically in Figure 9-2. The actual rate of growth is plotted on the horizontal axis; and the product of the "intended" or ex ante propensity to save and $\sigma$ is plotted on the vertical axis. Equilibrium growth occurs at some point where the two are equal (their equality being represented by the 45-degree line from the origin). Suppose $AB$ is the variable saving propensity plotted as an increasing function of $\dot{Y}$. Then the intersection of $AB$ with the 45-degree line at $E$ is the point of equilibrium growth. At $E$, the

FIGURE 9-2. *The Propensity to Save and the Rate of Income Growth*

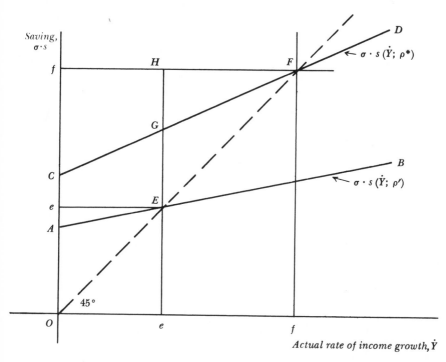

Source: Derived from equation 9-5 in the text.

actual rate of growth in income generates desired saving that is just sufficient to support the investment necessary to maintain that rate of growth. The economy continues to grow at rate *e* indefinitely.

It would perhaps be worthwhile to explore the stability properties of this equilibrium position a little further. If actual growth were arbitrarily set at zero, so as to eliminate the portfolio effect, then the saving propensity would still be positive and equal to *OA* (divided by σ) in Figure 9-2. If this saving were successfully translated into net investment, the rate of growth would be driven upward. However, to ensure that *AB* intersects the 45-degree line, so that an equilibrium like point *E* exists, *AB* must be constrained to having a slope of less than unity. That is, to prevent explosive growth in the context of the model, it is necessary that

(9-6) $$\partial s / \partial \dot{Y} < 1/\sigma.$$

Intuitively, it is easy to see that this last condition, which puts an upper bound on the portfolio effect, is not very stringent. Suppose that the output/capital ratio, $\sigma$, is $1/3$—as is commonly assumed. Then condition 9-6 implies that a 1 percentage point increase in $\dot{Y}$ can raise the propensity to save by 3 percentage points without inducing explosive growth. Hence, the portfolio effect of growth on savings can be quite large before our Harrod-Domar economy becomes unstable.

So far, $\rho$ has been assumed to be constant in focusing on the relationship between $\dot{Y}$ and $s$ along $AB$. That is, the implicit financial structure of the economy has been taken as given. One purpose of constructing this growth model, however, is to portray the consequences of a marked change in financial policy of the kind observed in some less developed countries. Let $\rho = \rho'$ represent financial "repression" with a low or negative real return on holding money and a small money–income ratio. Our saving function $AB$ is correspondingly low and reflects this repression. Now introduce a sharp increase in the real return on money that lifts the money–GNP ratio sharply. This financial reform is represented within the model by an increase in the parameter $\rho$ from $\rho'$ to $\rho^*$ so as to raise the saving function from $AB$ to $CD$ in Figure 9-2. Two effects on saving can then be identified: (1) the saving function as a whole shifts upward, and (2) its slope with respect to $\dot{Y}$ increases.

Each effect has a very interesting economic interpretation. With the rise in savings from $AB$ to $CD$, the equilibrium rate of growth increases sharply from $e$ to $f$, as measured on either axis. This can be partitioned into two constituent components. The buoyant effect of financial change on the propensity to save, before $\dot{Y}$ actually begins to rise, is captured in the movement from $E$ to $G$; whereas $GH$ is the *further increment to saving induced when $\dot{Y}$ rises to its new equilibrium level.* Geometrically, this last boost to saving or "growth dividend" is determined by the upward slope of $CD$, which reflects the impact of growth on the propensity to save after the monetary reform has occurred. (The slope of $CD$ is steeper than that of $AB$ because of the greater willingness of individuals to hold monetary assets once financial repression is released.)

Crude and highly aggregated as it is, our modified Harrod-

Domar model provides additional insight into why a discrete improvement in monetary policy can have such a sharp impact on observed growth and saving rates in such countries as Korea and Taiwan. The rise in desired holdings of real money balances not only stimulates saving directly but, once growth begins, channels even more saving through "organized" financial processes. Apart from monetary reform, however, the portfolio effect is undoubtedly important in permitting rapidly growing economies like the Japanese to sustain an extraordinarily high propensity to save over a prolonged period of time. In summary, a healthy financial system seems necessary for "reverse causation" (for growth to influence saving) to be a significant economic phenomenon even though it is difficult to quantify econometrically. Although no formal attempt at quantification was made in the statistical analysis of Chapter 8, this omission should not be construed as downgrading the importance of the portfolio effect.

# 10

## Fiscal Policy and the Liberalization of Foreign Trade

ALTHOUGH FINANCIAL REPRESSION is pervasive in the underdeveloped world, its critical importance is still not appreciated by government officials, academicians, or international agencies. In contrast, equally repressive foreign trade policies have come to the forefront of public consciousness in recent years. The record of extensive and often capricious government intervention in international flows of goods and services has been chronicled by the Organisation for Economic Co-operation and Development (OECD)[1] and by the International Bank for Reconstruction and Development (IBRD).[2] Import tariffs, licenses, quotas, advance deposits on imports, export retentions based on official selling prices, special exemptions from any of the above for favored producers, complex multiple rate categories for foreign exchange, outright

1. See the following studies, all published for the Development Centre of the Organisation for Economic Co-operation and Development by the Oxford University Press (London): Joel Bergsman, *Brazil: Industrialization and Trade Policies* (1970); Timothy King, *Mexico: Industrialization and Trade Policies since 1940* (1970); Jagdish N. Bhagwati and Padma Desai, *India, Planning for Industrialization: Industrialization and Trade Policies since 1951* (1970); Stephen R. Lewis, Jr., *Pakistan: Industrialization and Trade Policies* (1970); John H. Power and Gerardo P. Sicat, *The Philippines: Industrialization and Trade Policies*, and Mo-huan Hsing, *Taiwan: Industrialization and Trade Policies*, both published in the same volume (1971); and a master volume summarizing the experience of all six (including Argentina)—Ian Little, Tibor Scitovsky, and Maurice Scott, *Industry and Trade in Some Developing Countries: A Comparative Study* (1970).

2. Bela Balassa and Associates, *The Structure of Protection in Developing Countries* (Johns Hopkins Press for the International Bank for Reconstruction and Development and the Inter-American Development Bank, 1971).

prohibitions on some imports and some exports, and so on have all contributed to bureaucratic confusion and to the inordinate cheapening of some tradable commodities while creating undue scarcity of others.

Domestic industry is protected both because competing foreign products are kept out and, equally important, intermediate products are artificially cheapened—exportables and importables that are used by favored domestic industries or exclusively licensed firms.

In retrospect, this strategy of industrializing through import substitution has been disappointing. The endemic economic fragmentation and lack of generalized productivity growth, that were of concern in Chapter 2, have been aggravated. The prospects of further autarkic development—at least for small and medium-sized economies—now seem quite limited, despite the euphoria that had been associated with import substitution in its earlier stages. The studies by the OECD and the IBRD both recognize that a substantial relaxation of import restrictions—coupled with a suitable devaluation in the exchange rate toward an equilibrium level—is necessary to expand exports and overcome the shortage of foreign exchange that most developing countries (except those with large untapped petroleum deposits) seem to face.

But this clearer official recognition of the adverse consequences of repressing foreign trade comes at the expense of increased intellectual uneasiness. After all, protection for import-substituting industries was heralded, not so long ago, for encouraging more rapid capital accumulation and the faster acquisition of modern industrial technology.[3] "Colonial" dependence on the production and export of primary commodities was to be eliminated as economic stagnation was overcome. If the complex bureaucratic machinery of import substitution is now to be tossed away, what will prevent regression toward the supposedly unfavorable patterns of growth or nongrowth that were characteristic of the post–World War II era?

3. The early enthusiasm for import substitution was shared not only by the officials who were in charge of granting tariff protection and import licenses, but also by influential academicians such as Albert O. Hirschman, in *The Strategy of Economic Development* (Yale University Press, 1958), and Hirschman again in "The Political Economy of Import-Substituting Industrialization in Latin America," *Quarterly Journal of Economics*, Vol. 82 (February 1968), pp. 1–32.

By now, at least some readers may agree that a vigorous domestic capital market, centered on the monetary system, can be a more efficient engine of economic development. Since economic arguments for restricting foreign trade presume that the domestic capital market isn't working (see Chapter 3), such arguments become superfluous and positively misleading once financial growth gets under way. Users of manufactured commodities no longer need to be taxed by tariffs in order to subsidize new domestic producers. Instead, new firms with good prospects will be able to borrow more easily. Similarly, exclusive licenses to import capital goods no longer serve any useful economic purpose in making it easier for their holders to attract financial capital. Rather than having their surplus expropriated by adverse terms of trade, farmers can be induced to save voluntarily by acquiring financial assets bearing high rates of return that reflect the true scarcity of capital. In short, financial liberalization causes restraints on foreign trade to lose some dubious virtues while retaining their well documented vices.

Suppose, therefore, that the case for free trade is clear when the domestic capital market is working freely. (The difficult problem of effecting a successful transition to a liberal trading environment by jettisoning the welter of trade restrictions currently in force is deferred to Chapter 11.) What role then remains for fiscal policy—particularly the tax structure—in sustaining free international trade and liberalized domestic finance[4] after such reforms have been undertaken?

The problem is by no means trivial. First, assuming a general withdrawal of tariffs, tax concessions, and other subventions for particular firms and industries, what kind of new tax system is called for? What indeed is a reasonably neutral tax structure for less developed countries, whose administrative capacity is quite limited and who must rely on indirect taxes in general, and those on foreign trade in particular, for raising revenue? Second, is tax neutrality between exporting and import substitution compatible with maintaining high revenue elasticity with respect to a rapidly grow-

---

4. This chapter concentrates wholly on the domestic financial system and foreign trade confined to goods and services. The role of international flows of capital is examined in Chapter 12.

ing national income? The analysis of optimum monetization showed the importance of avoiding a weak fiscal policy that would force the government to borrow from the central bank. This chapter presents a rough sketch of a tax policy that would satisfy both the neutrality and the elasticity criteria.

## *Tax Neutrality and the Wellsprings of Export Revival*

To strive for tax neutrality seems singularly unexciting—a game only an economist could enjoy. But because of the extreme anti-protectionist policy the less developed countries have followed in the export sectors of their economies, a less discriminatory policy can have a far-reaching impact on export expansion. An understanding of this consequence of trade liberalization is important in order to forestall a new battery of fiscal and financial subsidies to promote exports that is designed to replace or to override the myriad of similar subventions now enjoyed by industries producing import substitutes. Mere neutrality in taxation and in providing financial services will suffice.

To understand this, one should know that the *implicit* taxation of export industries is usually much greater than the visible direct restraints on actual export flows.[5] In fact, the main tax on exports arises from the ways in which tariff and quota restrictions on imports operate through the foreign exchanges to reduce the profitability of exporting. Keeping imports out reduces the effective demand for, and consequently the price of, foreign exchange relative to the domestic costs of labor, capital, intermediate inputs, and so

---

5. However, direct restrictions or unusually heavy taxation of exports have been surprisingly prevalent. Raw jute and cotton exports have been taxed in Pakistan to promote the domestic production of jute and cotton textiles. The export of iron ore from Brazil or India may be restricted for the benefit of the local steel industry. Even within India, the export of food grains from surplus states to deficit states is frequently prohibited for the benefit of consumers in the former. The fall in exports from Brazil (other than coffee) through the 1950s up to the early 1960s was, in part, due to taxes and other quantitative restrictions on exports. See, for example, Nathaniel H. Leff, "Export Stagnation and Autarkic Development in Brazil, 1947–1962," *Quarterly Journal of Economics*, Vol. 81 (May 1967), pp. 286–301.

on that producers of export products must pay. Since exporters sell in foreign markets at this less favorable "real" exchange rate, they are caught in a profit squeeze, which reduces traditional exports and blocks new export development—particularly of manufactures. More formally, one can show that a uniform tariff of $X$ percent on all imports is equivalent to an alternative policy of imposing a uniform tax of $X$ percent on all exports,[6] in the sense that the allocation of resources within the domestic economy would be the same under either policy.

In Table 10-1 tariffs on imports in 1962 in the European Economic Community (EEC) are compared with those in major Latin American countries: Argentina, Brazil, Chile, Colombia, and Mexico. The data include special import surcharges, multiple exchange rates, advance deposits required on imports, as well as tariffs, and their sum is much higher in the Latin American countries than in Europe (or the United States if it were shown). In Latin America, tariff rates average over 200 percent on consumable imports and then are scaled down to an average of "only" 50 to 70 percent on industrial materials and capital goods. Even higher and more differentiated restrictions on imports exist in India, Pakistan, and Ceylon, although complex quotas and exchange controls make equivalent tariff calculations less meaningful. If such heavy restraints on imports are equivalent to taxing exports at the same effective rates, one would hardly be surprised if exports from LDCs fared badly in the postwar period.

Table 10-2 indicates roughly the relative export performance of LDCs that are now semi-industrial because of the import-substitution strategies they have followed in the past. The growth in total exports of those countries that are generally referred to as "developed"[7] is a useful benchmark for measuring the growth of the international economy as a whole. Total gross exports of these

6. For a formal proof of this proposition, under conditions reasonably expected to hold in the long run, see Ronald I. McKinnon, "Intermediate Products and Differential Tariffs: A Generalization of Lerner's Symmetry Theorem," *Quarterly Journal of Economics*, Vol. 80 (November 1966), pp. 584–615, which elaborated on an earlier paper by A. P. Lerner, "The Symmetry Between Import and Export Taxes," *Economica*, Vol. 3 (August 1936), pp. 306–13.

7. Industrial Western Europe, the United States, Canada, Australia, and New Zealand are included. Japan is excluded from this reference group and is tabulated separately.

TABLE 10-1. *Tariffs and Other Charges on Imports of Consumer Goods and Intermediate Products in Five Latin American Countries and the European Economic Community, 1962*
Percent

| Type of import | Argen- tina | Brazil | Chile | Colom- bia | Mexico | European Economic Com- munity |
|---|---|---|---|---|---|---|
| *Consumer goods* | | | | | | |
| Nonprocessed foodstuffs (13 products) | 123 | 264 | 46 | 185 | 65 | 21 |
| Durable consumer goods (11 products) | 266 | 328 | 90 | 108 | 147 | 19 |
| Current consumer manufactures (31 products) | 176 | 260 | 328 | 247 | 114 | 17 |
| Consumer goods, average (55 products) | 181 | 275 | 214 | 205 | 109 | 18 |
| *Intermediate products* | | | | | | |
| Industrial raw materials (10 products) | 55 | 106 | 111 | 57 | 38 | 1 |
| Semimanufactured goods, including fuels (32 products) | 95 | 80 | 98 | 28 | 28 | 7 |
| Capital goods (28 products) | 98 | 84 | 45 | 18 | 14 | 13 |
| Intermediate products, average (70 products) | 90 | 85 | 79 | 28 | 24 | 9 |
| *Overall average, consumer goods and intermediate products* (125 products) | 131 | 169 | 138 | 106 | 61 | 13 |

Source: United Nations, *Economic Bulletin for Latin America*, Vol. 9 (March 1964), Table 5, p. 75.

mature economies increased by 295 percent from 1953 to 1970,[8] thus indicating trading opportunities that rivaled the "golden era" prior to 1914. However, most semiindustrial LDCs have failed to avail themselves of these trading possibilities, and their exports have grown much more slowly.

8. The 1953–70 period was chosen because it begins well after the recovery from the Second World War. The value of exports is measured in undeflated U.S. dollars simply because no satisfactory single price deflator exists. One should keep in mind, however, that the prices of goods entering foreign trade have been rising much more slowly than domestic cost-of-living indices.

TABLE 10-2. *Exports of Developed and Semiindustrial Underdeveloped Economies, 1953, 1962, and 1970*
Millions of current U.S. dollars

| Country | Exports[a] 1953 | 1962 | 1970 | Percentage change, 1953–70 |
|---|---|---|---|---|
| *Developed economies*[b] | 49,250 | 85,715 | 194,671 | +295.3 |
| *Less developed countries with slowly growing foreign trade* | | | | |
| Argentina | 1,125 | 1,216 | 1,773 | +57.6 |
| Brazil | 1,539 | 1,214 | 2,739 | +78.0 |
| Colombia | 596 | 463 | 732 | +22.8 |
| Uruguay | 270 | 153 | 233 | −13.7 |
| Venezuela | 1,445 | 2,594 | 2,660 | +84.1 |
| India | 1,114 | 1,399 | 2,006 | +80.1 |
| Pakistan | 438 | 422 | 717 | +63.7 |
| Ceylon | 329 | 379 | 341 | +3.6 |
| Turkey | 396 | 381 | 465 | +17.4 |
| *Less developed countries with moderate trade growth* | | | | |
| Chile | 408 | 530 | 1,247 | +205.6 |
| Mexico | 595 | 913 | 1,403 | +135.8 |
| Peru | 219 | 538 | 1,044 | +376.7 |
| Philippines | 398 | 556 | 1,062 | +166.8 |
| Thailand | 272 | 457 | 703 | +158.5 |
| *Rapidly growing economies* | | | | |
| Japan | 1,272 | 4,941 | 19,447 | +1,428.9 |
| China (Taiwan) | 128 | 218 | 1,428 | +1,015.6 |
| Korea | 40 | 55 | 835 | +1,418.2[c] |

Sources: International Monetary Fund, *International Financial Statistics*, Vol. 25 (May 1972), Vol. 23 (January 1970), and *Supplement to 1967/68 Issues*.
a. The narrow definition of commodity exports in dollars is used, with services excluded.
b. Includes the industrialized countries of Western Europe, Australia, Canada, New Zealand, and the United States; excludes Japan, which is included in the last group.
c. Calculated for 1962–70 only because the Korean war was still going on in 1953.

Latin American countries as a whole did badly, with the first five in Table 10-2—Argentina, Brazil, Colombia, Uruguay, and Venezuela—doing astonishingly poorly. Colombia had less than one-tenth the export growth of the advanced countries, and Uruguay's was actually negative. Brazil, which has half of the population of South America, had a 78 percent increase in the dollar volume of its exports, which is only about one-fourth of the growth experienced by mature industrial countries. Venezuela's growth rate of 84 percent, the highest in this lagging group, was largely petroleum-based and not indicative of broad development.

Export malaise is not confined to Latin America. India, Pakistan, Ceylon, and Turkey all have poor export performance records, as may be seen in Table 10-2. Indian trade expansion has been a little more than one-fourth of that achieved by the mature industrial economies and has been negligible compared to the export growth of Japan and Taiwan. The Pakistani export performance in the late 1960s, just prior to its civil war, was better than it was in the late 1950s, but is still very disappointing over all. Ceylon's export earnings are quite unstable, and growth has been negligible since 1953. Turkey's very low export growth rate (17 percent) can be explained by its extremely stringent foreign exchange controls on imports.

On the other hand, Taiwan and Korea provide examples of a much more rapid rise in volume of exports, which was associated with marked internal transformation. In the short interval from 1962 to 1970, Taiwan's exports increased from 13.2 percent of gross national product to 31.1 percent and Korea's from 5.2 percent to 15.0 percent. Since the reforms of 1964–65, Korea has managed to maintain the extraordinary export growth rate of almost 40 percent a year, whereas exports were quite moribund for the preceding ten years. There were no apparent external barriers to rapid export development in these two countries (or in Japan); both economies were able to undertake major internal structural shifts toward exporting within a relatively short period of time.

Should the slowly growing semi-industrial LDCs sharply reorient their policies away from import substitution toward export expansion? Surprisingly, in one important sense the answer is no. It is indeed tempting to try to compensate for past suppression of exports, which is perhaps still reflected in an unduly low domestic price of foreign currency, by shifting the panoply of fiscal and financial incentives toward exporters while leaving antecedent distortions more or less untouched.

A prime example of such partial compensation is the export bonus scheme introduced by the government of Pakistan in 1959.

Producers of some manufactured exports were no longer required to surrender all their foreign exchange proceeds at the official exchange rate. Rather, a portion of the foreign exchange earnings—the portion varying from one industry to another—could be kept and resold to a select group of importers at a much higher price. In effect, a multiple exchange-rate system was introduced (similar to many Latin American schemes) to get some relief from obvious exchange-rate overvaluation. However, the subsidy varied enormously among manufactured exports, since some exporters had access to imported intermediate materials at the low official price and others did not. Such discriminatory treatment, of course, preserves differences in social rates of return to capital. It may also markedly reduce the net foreign exchange earnings of some industries.

> The rate of effective subsidy to these industries is exceedingly high. Even if the calculations had an extremely large margin of error, one could hardly avoid the conclusion that perhaps half of the value added in the export industries was only apparent, and not real, and that the gross earnings of foreign exchange from the Export Bonus industries must substantially overstate the net export earnings of the scheme.[9]

Another common technique is to rebate indirect taxes and tariffs levied at earlier production stages on industrial supplies used by exporters as well as exempting them from any direct tax liability. The bureaucratic machinery for calculating bona fide rebates is usually cumbersome and inefficient. But in addition, India subsidized exporters by giving them entitlements (licenses) to import twice the import content of their exports, subject to a maximum of 75 percent of the f.o.b. value of their exports, with various exceptions to the maximums.[10] Because of the unduly low price they paid for foreign exchange, coupled with stringent import rationing, the "surplus" supplies could be resold in domestic markets at prices far higher than the import cost. This introduced highly discriminatory subsidies and encouraged export activities with low real value added and high dependence on imported supplies.

It is common practice in LDCs (and many advanced countries) to give exporters of manufactures special access to central or com-

9. Lewis, *Pakistan: Industrialization and Trade Policies*, pp. 130–31.
10. See Bhagwati and Desai, *India*, pp. 406–13.

mercial bank credit at low real rates of interest. Insofar as these low or negative rates are passed back to depositors, this contributes to the general financial repression mentioned earlier. Where capital is very scarce, it is important that exporters (along with all other producers) have abundant credit, but at rates of interest high enough to reflect the scarcity of capital.

Fortunately such specialized fiscal and financial compensation for individual exporters is unnecessary. If existing protective tariffs and quota restrictions on imports were generally eliminated, an enormous implicit burden on exporting activities would be lifted, and at the same time more neutral resource allocation would result.

## *Indirect Taxation and the Problem of Revenue Inelasticity*

Developing countries rely heavily on a wide variety of indirect taxes that are not applied uniformly. Sales taxes, turnover taxes, license fees, stamp fees, customs duties, excises, and so on coexist in uneasy profusion. In the poorer countries, almost two-thirds of all tax revenue comes from sources other than direct taxation of income or property. (See Table 10-3.) Probably Table 10-3 understates the dependence of the LDCs on indirect taxation because various export taxes are excluded as are business "income" taxes, which are sometimes assessed as if they were sales or turnover taxes.[11] Of the total revenue from indirect taxation, well over one-half comes from foreign trade—not only from customs duties but from various sales taxes that fall disproportionately heavily on imported commodities. It is assumed here that for administrative reasons most poor countries will remain heavily dependent on indirect taxes[12] in general and on those that fall on the highly visible foreign trade sector in particular.

11. This is because business accounting systems may be primitive or nonexistent. The tax assessor frequently cannot calculate profit or net business income directly in order to establish the tax base. Hence, some estimate of gross sales—with a standard markup—may be used instead to establish "income" for the tax assessor's purposes.

12. Personal income taxation can and should be greatly improved in most countries, both to equalize the distribution of income and to raise more revenue. However, it seems unlikely that most LDCs have the administrative capability to make the personal income tax a major source of revenue in the near future.

TABLE 10-3. *Reliance of the Developing Countries and the Highly Developed Countries on Indirect Taxes and Customs Duties, by Per Capita Gross National Product Class, 1968*[a]

| Per capita GNP class (in U.S. dollars) | Number of countries | Indirect taxes as percentage of total tax revenue | Customs duties as percentage of total tax revenue[b] |
|---|---|---|---|
| Developing countries | | | |
| 100 or less | 20 | 68 | 35 (*41*) |
| 101–200 | 11 | 64 | 32[c] (*39*) |
| 201–500 | 19 | 64 | 33[d] (*35*) |
| 501–850 | 9 | 50 | 18 |
| Highly developed countries | | | |
| Over 850 | 15 | 32 | 4 |

Source: John F. Due, *Indirect Taxation in Developing Economies: The Role and Structure of Customs Duties, Excises, and Sales Taxes* (Johns Hopkins Press, 1970), Table 1-1, p. 2; and Table 2-1, p. 28.

a. Data are for the latest year available during the 1965–69 period, 1968 in most instances.

b. Figures in parentheses give percentages for total collections at customs, including sales tax revenue collected at importation.

c. Nine countries; customs duty collections were not segregated from other collections at customs for two of the eleven countries.

d. Eighteen countries; customs duty collections were not segregated from other collections at customs for one of the nineteen countries.

An unfortunate consequence of import substitution is that revenue from the indirect tax system as a whole has become *less income-elastic*. As gross national product (GNP) grows, revenue from indirect taxes tends to grow less than proportionately. The problem, however, is not with indirect taxation per se, but with the way it has been distorted to provide incentives for industrialization to replace imports.

Some loss of tax revenue and tax elasticity occurs more or less by accident or by indirection. Most LDCs were, in the not too distant past, producers of primary commodities only, many of which were exported. Because of their large subsistence sectors, perhaps nonmonetized, tariffs on imported manufactures were the principal levies for raising revenue. Moreover, to try to achieve more progressivity in the tax structure, imports of consumer manufactures (luxuries) like cosmetics, perfumes, refrigerators, processed foods, and so on were heavily taxed. Domestic production of similar goods was so insignificant as to escape even *pro forma* taxation. In Ethiopia, which has yet to industrialize significantly, more than 200 of its 254 positive *ad valorem* tariffs were imposed for revenue purposes, not to protect domestic production. With import weights, the average of these 200 tariffs is about 35 percent, with some ranging as high as 60 percent.

Obviously as Ethiopia matures and capital becomes available for industrialization, these revenue tariffs of long standing become protective and can attract domestic resources into the manufacture of these same consumer "luxuries." (This was not a problem in the earlier, more pristine state.) The government then loses revenue as the volume of imports of final consumer goods is reduced when domestic manufacture begins. The tax system has become inelastic to the rising income that is associated with industrialization.

However, most revenue losses in LDCs are the direct result of more purposeful public policies. High or virtually prohibitive tariffs imposed for protective reasons on consumer goods—for example, the 200 percent tariffs shown for Latin American countries in Table 10-1—do not raise any revenue as the import base dries up. In many situations, they simply supersede more moderate revenue tariffs. Quota restrictions or prohibitions on imports reduce revenues further when the restrictions fall on commodities that are nominally dutiable.

Less often realized, however, is the importance of tariff and other tax *concessions* to newly protected industries in contributing to the inelasticity of tax revenues. These can take the form of simply excusing particular producers from paying customs duties or other sales taxes on their imported supplies and capital goods. Alternatively, the formal tariff or sales tax rate may simply be set at zero on certain classes of imported commodities considered to be important inputs into industrial development. In Ethiopia, which is not particularly far along in this process, revenue losses from both kinds of concessions on tariffs and sales taxes were over 40 percent of revenue actually collected from imports.[13] Moreover, the proportion of revenue lost has grown rapidly since conscious industrialization began. In Latin America, India, and Pakistan the value of such concessions is harder to calculate because of the disequilibrium in their exchange rates and the need for compensating tariffs. Yet in many cases, Korea in 1966 for example, the reve-

13. Taking the pattern of imports observed in 1970 as given, that is, as invariant to the structure of tariffs and exemptions.

nue lost from exempting particular importers from tax was greater than the revenue actually collected from taxing imports.

Because government expenditures *are* elastic to income growth even if revenues are not, the problem of relieving financial repression is made much more difficult. Growth brings with it a tendency toward budgetary deficits. Public saving does not keep pace, and governments either allow more non-neutral small taxes to proliferate or turn to central banks for financing, given the absence of capital markets for absorbing long-term public debt. Excessive issue of nominal money can then cause inflation and a reduction in the real stock of money, as was pointed out earlier. Building more revenue elasticity into a reformed tax system is necessary in order to avoid financial repression. Fortunately the structure of indirect taxes can be changed so as to increase revenue, even as discrimination within and against foreign trade is reduced.

## *From Tariffs to the Value Added Tax*

Suppose the minister of finance is given a broad mandate to reform the whole structure of indirect taxation as financial reforms are put into effect. He sweeps away the maze of highly differentiated tariffs and quotas designed to restrict foreign trade and, simultaneously, dispenses with all the many tariff and tax exemptions enjoyed by favored domestic producers. Finally, to be completely fanciful, suppose that the minister declares himself willing to rationalize existing turnover taxes, excises, license fees, export retentions, payroll taxes, and so on, imposed at some or all of the various stages of production and distribution. What then would an optimal tax structure look like? (Difficult transitional problems, particularly the maintenance of equilibrium in the foreign exchanges, are examined in Chapter 11.)

A moderate uniform tariff of, say, 10 to 20 percent on all imports—from which there were no exemptions—would be one way to maintain revenue as income grows. The administrative importance of including "organized" foreign trade activity in the tax base—with only a moderate symmetrical general burden on exporting—is recognized. In addition, particular natural resource exports, such as copper, oil, coffee, and so on, could have their own form of severance taxes, each optimally tailored to reflect inelastic foreign demand, international commodity agreements, or economic "rents" inherent in the mineral vein or oil pool being tapped. It is assumed here that these last highly specific taxes will be included in any newly reformed tax structure.

While a uniform tariff system for foreign trade would be a great improvement for most LDCs, it would not be a "first-best" solution because inconsistencies with other taxes would remain. Should domestic producers be given credit for the tariff paid on imported supplies against their own domestic sales or income tax liability? More particularly, should exporters get tariff drawbacks on the imported supplies they use? If so, rebates from taxes paid on domestic supplies sold to exporters may also be necessary in order to avoid bias against local firms. Fortunately the introduction of a *uniform* value added tax (VAT) can overcome these difficulties by combining the simplicity of a single *ad valorem* levy on imports with generally neutral taxation of domestic and foreign commodities destined for final consumption.

First, how would the VAT be administered in the absence of foreign trade? The tax base of "value added" can be defined in more than one way. Starting from a tabulation of gross sales, the taxpaying firm can subtract *all* supplies purchased—including capital goods as well as raw and semifinished materials—in calculating its tax base; or the value of capital assets purchased can be disallowed and a depreciation allowance substituted. There are significant administrative advantages in choosing the former "consumption" version of the VAT rather than the latter "net-product" version.[14] First, it is always difficult to distinguish capital goods from current inputs in an accounting sense; and, when that is done, it is even more difficult to designate an unbiased system of depreciation accounting. These issues require the services of bat-

14. A more detailed analysis of this distinction and of the VAT generally may be found in Mel Krauss and Richard M. Bird, "The Value Added Tax: Critique of a Review," *Journal of Economic Literature,* Vol. 9 (December 1971), pp. 1167–73; and in Harry Johnson and Mel Krauss, "Border Taxes, Border Tax Adjustments, Comparative Advantage, and the Balance of Payments," *Canadian Journal of Economics,* Vol. 3 (November 1970), pp. 595–602. Problems of introducing the VAT in a particular less developed country are discussed in Ronald I. McKinnon, "Export Expansion Through Tax Policy: The Case for a Value-Added Tax in Singapore," *Malayan Economic Review,* Vol. 11 (October 1966), pp. 1–27.

teries of tax lawyers and accountants in economies like the United States with large firms and relatively sophisticated accounting systems. For the much smaller enterprises in the underdeveloped countries it would be particularly costly if such fine bookkeeping distinctions were required. Indeed, these accounting difficulties have so undermined attempts to tax corporate profits or net income in many LDCs that the corporate income tax may itself be replaced by a comprehensive VAT.

Once the decision is made to use the "consumption" version of the VAT, with a single rate, say 15 percent, then the tax assessor has a relatively simple task. "Value added" refers to the sum of wages, salaries, profits, interest, and rents generated within the firm, which are all to be taxed at the same rate. Fortunately the tax collector does *not* have to know or estimate these individually. All he has to verify is the dollar value of the gross sales of the firm, which is a relatively easy business statistic to obtain. The taxpayer has to supply evidence of materials purchased from other firms that have already been taxed. The tax base then is simply the *difference* between gross sales and the value of those inputs whose purchase from suppliers can be verified.

For an open economy, another decision would have to be made as to whether the VAT should be applied on the "origin" principle or on the "destination" principle. The distinction lies basically in the form of the *border-tax adjustment* chosen to reconcile the taxation of imports and exports, with the VAT system imposed on domestic goods. (This assumes that the "consumption" version of the VAT would be used domestically.) The authorities could, under the origin principle, choose to tax *all* domestic production, including exports, at the factory gate. Because of the symmetry between the export and import taxes analyzed above, this origin principle would then require that imports *not* be taxed as they enter the economy so as to maintain neutrality with respect to foreign trade.

While it would be acceptable in certain circumstances, the VAT administered on the origin principle would not be desirable in LDCs because no explicit taxation would occur at the import stage. LDCs have a long history of levying taxes on imports at ports and border-crossing stations because of the relatively high visibility and sophisticated nature of international commerce. In fact the most primitive economies may be administratively capable of taxing little else. Fortunately a VAT levied on the *destination* principle could incorporate a uniform *ad valorem* tax on all imports as an integral part of a conceptually neutral tax system. As the tariff and quota structure is dismantled, customs officials can avoid technological unemployment by collecting the new 15 percent border-tax adjustment for the VAT on all goods entering the economy. But if imports as well as domestic output were to be taxed under the destination principle, neutrality would require that exports be exempted from the VAT in order to avoid double taxation of foreign trade. It would be a straightforward matter to credit users of imported goods with having paid the VAT border-tax adjustment and systematically to exempt exporters and their suppliers from the VAT.

Not only would there be a zero tax on value added by the final exporter, but rebates would be given for taxes that had been paid earlier on supplies that were purchased, so that the whole product would be exempted. Domestic supplies would be put on the same basis as imports in this respect. This systematic tax relief is inherently part of the machinery of the VAT, and no special ad hoc tax adjustments for exporters would be necessary or desirable. Under a tariff system, on the other hand, an arrangement for rebating tariffs paid on the imported supplies used by exporters would not be neutral because of the bias it would create against using domestic materials, which are subject to other forms of taxation, in export activities. This bias would be avoided if the VAT replaced import duties as a source of revenue and protective tariffs were eliminated.

But what about the inevitable pressure for special exemptions from the VAT for some imported industrial materials and capital goods? Fortunately domestic producers would feel less need to seek exemptions because credit for the VAT levied on imported supplies could be systematically carried forward as an offset against the VAT liability on the firm's own sales. In contrast, under a high and differentiated tariff structure, domestic producers who did *not* get full tariff exemptions on imported supplies might well find their competitive position quite hopeless, both domestically and internationally. Authorities would be in a much better position, therefore, to withstand pressure for tax concessions under a comprehensive, but uniform, VAT system.

The administration of the VAT could be simply structured with, say, only two major collection points—where goods are imported and where domestic and foreign products are sold at the wholesale level; or, the administration could easily be extended to include gross sales of major firms, whether at the wholesale level or not; or it could be extended further to cover small and medium-sized firms. The choice would depend on whether the tax authorities wanted to commit further resources to administering the tax and how much additional revenue would be gained. If some commodities were missed at the import stage through smuggling, they could effectively be taxed at later manufacturing or wholesaling stages. For most LDCs, the reverse administrative problem exists: goods must be taxed at the import stage because tax collection is inefficient within the domestic economy but relatively effective at its borders.

In general, it is not feasible or desirable in most LDCs—or even in such European countries as France—to extend the tax to include the final retail stage of distribution, where collection of the tax would be costly because of the multitude of peddlers, vendors, and very small merchants. France has adopted the expedient of exempting the last 20 percent of value added in products sold to final consumers. This eliminates most small retailers from any legal tax liability under the VAT. In addition, basic unprocessed foods are often exempted so that farmers are excused from legal tax liability, and food prices are kept low. Essentially, the VAT is best considered as a systematic method of taxing "modern" industrial commodities, while certain agricultural and service activities are best handled by other forms of taxation.

To summarize the merits of the VAT in facilitating a general tax liberalization to support the liberalization of financial processes described earlier:

Within the extensive set of industrial activities actually covered by the tax net, the VAT is conceptually neutral in that (1) differential commodity or multiple taxation is avoided, (2) foreign trade is taxed on a par with domestic value added, and (3) all the primary factors of production bear the same rate of tax.

One would expect revenue from the VAT to be *highly elastic* to rising income—even with a uniform tax rate. The tax base is tied to the more rapidly growing modern sector and, it is hoped, to liberalized foreign trade. The pressure for special exemptions and concessions associated with import-substituting industrialization is reduced because of the coherent nature of the tax itself.

Since the administratively tractable "consumption" version of the VAT excludes capital accumulation (saving) from the tax base, investment incentives arising out of a successful financial liberalization are augmented. One shortcoming of the VAT, however, is that it is not a suitable vehicle for effecting significant income redistribution from the rich to the poor, except perhaps insofar as it permits distortions in foreign trade and special tax concessions to be eliminated.

## From Tariffs to Consumer Excises

Another complementary tax device with potentially more redistributive implications might be considered briefly. The VAT would fall on all imports, including intermediate inputs and capital goods, which are now exempted. These intermediate products would be subject to no further tax. However, much higher tariffs on consumer "luxuries" are still imposed for revenue purposes and for taxing relatively high income groups within LDCs. These levies on automobiles, toys, jewelry, air conditioners, and so on, can give substantial progressivity to the tax system, whereas a uniform VAT levy of say 15 percent would not. (There are many consumption taxes, for example, the tax on cigarettes, that may be regressive.) Since personal income taxation may be quite ineffective, there is a good case for continuing to tax consumer luxuries at different rates appropriate for each commodity, in addition to the uniform VAT levy.

In order to avoid unintended protection for domestic producers of consumer luxuries, however, countries should convert revenue tariffs to consumer excises. These excises would be collected by customs officials on imports, but domestic producers of luxury goods would also become liable at the same rate, with the tax collected at the "factory gate." This excise technique of taxing final consumers avoids bias against foreign trade in the process of indus-trialization, and it also maintains or increases overall revenue elasticity as consumption and income grow. The degree of rate differentiation among individual consumption goods would de-pend on:

• the consequences for income distribution,
• the price elasticity of demand and the resulting revenue the government might expect,
• the enforcement problem, including incentives given to smug-glers, and
• the historical level of the equivalent revenue tariff.

Needless to say, this conversion of revenue tariffs to consumer excises would not be difficult for those consumer goods that are not yet produced domestically in any great quantity. On the other hand, for consumer goods that are produced domestically as well as being imported, the conversion should be made in conjunction with a general removal of tariffs and quotas on *all* imports. The resulting depreciation of the foreign exchange value of the domes-tic currency then lightens the burden on domestic industries as they adjust to losing their tariff protection and become liable for these consumer excises and the VAT. It could be a serious mistake to try to convert one industry at a time. The whole problem of effecting the transition to a liberal foreign trade and financial policy is treated more comprehensively in Chapter 11.

## Concluding Comment

What would remain of the tariff structure and quota restrictions once these conversions to the VAT and to consumer excise taxa-tion were completed? It is possible to imagine an economy with no tariffs and quotas at all, even though foreign trade would con-tribute fully to the tax base from both an administrative and a revenue point of view. This wholly neutral tax policy might well be optimal if financial liberalization and the development of a thriving capital market could be secured. Alternatively, a very limited number of protective tariffs, but not quotas or quantitative restrictions, might be retained for new industries. However, these should be systematically phased out as industries matured, so that the economy would show no net increase in the number of tariffs as time passed.

Even modest protection to a few industries, however, necessarily implies modest antiprotection to others. The unfortunate historical precedents for such discriminatory trade policy are so unfavorable that governments may rationally choose to tie their own hands against granting new protection once a general reform is secured. This could be facilitated if LDCs became more fully participating members of the General Agreement on Tariffs and Trade and waived their rights under Article 18 to unilaterally impose tariffs or quotas on imports for "development" purposes. Such a waiver would strengthen the bargaining position of LDCs within GATT for securing tariff concessions—under the most-favored-nation principle—from advanced industrial nations. However, the main restraints on foreign trade originate within LDCs themselves, and these domestic restraints must remain the principal target of economic reform.

# 11

# The Transition: Exchange-Rate Flexibility and the Role of Foreign Capital

*So every bondman in his own hand bears*
*The power to cancel his captivity.*

—Shakespeare, *Julius Caesar*

SINCE ECONOMIC POLICY falls short of good practice reasonably considered, it is perhaps surprising that the postwar economic history of less developed countries (LDCs) shows so many attempts to secure greater liberalization, both in foreign trade and in domestic finance and fiscal policy. More often than not, these reforming countries have received advice and financial support from the International Monetary Fund (IMF), the International Bank for Reconstruction and Development (IBRD), and other multinational lending consortia composed of creditors from the advanced industrial nations. Indeed, substantial net inflows of foreign capital including "stabilization" loans have been used frequently.

Yet most policy changes toward greater liberalization have been partial and short-lived. Not all fiscal and financial distortions are experienced in a severe form by any one country, but then few countries succeed in escaping all of them on a sustained basis. Unfortunately, regression is a common phenomenon.

## Some Unhappy Evidence from Past Reforms

During the 1950s and 1960s, several of the developing countries undertook to curb inflation through tighter monetary and fiscal controls, with mixed results.

*Chile.* In the late 1950s, Chile suffered from high inflation (see Table 8-5) coupled with economic stagnation. A change in policy to curb inflation, readjust exchange rates, and liberalize imports was implemented in 1959 with the help of a substantial increase in foreign aid and net supplier credits from abroad. Inflation was stopped for almost three years (1959–61), and industrial production increased modestly as imports rose. A prohibition on the importation of some seven hundred different commodities, announced on January 12, 1962, rather dramatically signaled the end of liberalized foreign trade. Inflation resumed in 1962 and has continued ever since.

*Brazil.* The attempt to curb inflation in Brazil from 1964 to 1967 brought on the industrial stagnation discussed in some detail in Chapter 7, although the accompanying policy toward foreign trade was more successful. It included the relaxation of import restrictions, capital inflows with debt rescheduling, and more continuous devaluations, which have offset internal inflation and sustained expanding exports after 1965. However, a partial reversal of import liberalization occurred at the end of 1968, when duties were increased on a wide variety of goods (mainly consumer goods) by 100 percentage points.[1] Although industrial output picked up in the early 1970s, inflation has continued—but with higher interest rates on some classes of bank deposits. Whether or not Brazil finally liberalizes completely, it is clear that the process has been painful and lengthy, with the possibility of regression ever present.

*Colombia.* In 1962 Colombia devalued its principal exchange rate for imports by 34 percent. Substantial import liberalization, the elimination of price controls, and tighter monetary and fiscal

---

1. Ian Little, Tibor Scitovsky, and Maurice Scott, *Industry and Trade in Some Developing Countries: A Comparative Study* (London: Oxford University Press for the Organisation for Economic Co-operation and Development, 1970), p. 380.

policy were to be undertaken as stipulated by the IMF. In return for such good behavior by Colombia:

> The impressive external aid offered in reward was to be channeled mainly through the Consultative Group, which was to be convened immediately to consider financing of $450 million worth of projects during the period up to the end of 1964. Total net long-term aid effectively utilizable was expected to reach $150 million in 1963 and more in subsequent years. This level implied more than doubling the 1961–62 average; in 1960 net long-term aid had been zero. Additionally, the IMF provided a new "stand-by" of $52.5 million, and commercial banks in the United States made available $40.5 million of acceptance credits.
>
> *The Aftermath.* In almost all respects the aftermath of the devaluation diverged dramatically from the projections. The price rise accelerated sharply. . . .
>
> Intervention by the Central Bank to maintain the rate of 10 [pesos to the dollar] proved far more costly than anticipated. In the first four months following the devaluation, almost all the IMF's stand-by had to be drawn, though the pressure then slackened. Demand for imports continued at high levels. Under these conditions the Colombian authorities found it impossible to liberalize imports. The new system of automatic and prior-approval lists constituted a more restrictive policy than that prevailing before the devaluation crisis developed.[2]

Another shortage of foreign exchange developed in 1964, again choking the flow of intermediate materials used by Colombian industry. Industrial stagnation contributed to severe social disorder. Similar promises of reform, accompanied by a devaluation and an external aid package of exceptional size, again took place in 1965. The new policy relieved the immediate shortages of imported inputs and encouraged some industrial expansion. However, sustained progress in curbing inflation and liberalizing foreign trade was not achieved—as a glance at Colombia's rather dismal export performance might indicate. (See Table 10-2.)

*Pakistan.* Besides the partial devaluation inherent in the export bonus scheme, described in Chapter 10, Pakistan received large inflows of foreign financial assistance over the 1959–64 period, including both grants and loans from a variety of international donors. Import liberalization in Pakistan was not associated with

2. Harold B. Dunkerley, "Exchange-Rate Systems in Conditions of Continuing Inflation—Lessons from Colombian Experience," in Gustav F. Papanek (ed.), *Development Policy—Theory and Practice* (Harvard University Press, 1968), pp. 127–28.

any devaluation in the official exchange rate, but there was progressive removal of quantitative restrictions on various classes of industrial imports, culminating in the introduction of a fairly lengthy "free list" in 1964. These increased imports, financed by aid inflows, did result in a significant dismantling of rationing and other severe administrative restrictions on the use of industrial materials and capital goods. However, as external aid tapered off and some of it had to be repaid, more stringent import controls were reimposed in the late 1960s. Little lasting change in the structure of foreign trade or in domestic propensities to save and invest seems to have been accomplished.

*Argentina.* In 1959 Argentina devalued its currency and terminated all import restrictions and price controls.

> Because the stabilization measures adopted at the time fell mainly on wages rather than profits and were accompanied by broad import-surcharge exemptions for imports of investment goods and efforts to attract foreign capital, the rapid recovery that followed was spurred mostly by an unprecedented investment boom. Imports rose by 37 percent between 1959 and 1960–61, almost half of the rise corresponding to increased purchases of capital goods. The resulting trade deficit did not create immediate balance-of-payments problems because it was offset by the inflow of foreign capital, a large share of which was short-term. This feature led to the collapse of the boom, beginning in the second half of 1961, when depressed export receipts resulting from a poor harvest obliged the Central Bank to sell large amounts of foreign exchange from its reserves to support the pegged rate. This development, combined with growing uncertainty over the future political stability of the country, undermined the confidence of foreign creditors. They began to recall their loans—a process that was accelerated after the government fell in March 1962.[3]

Besides another industrial recession, this episode left Argentina with an overhang of $3 billion of foreign debt in 1963 and immediate annual debt service charges of about 7 percent of gross national product at 1963 prices. It is still too early to assess the consequences of greater exchange flexibility (more frequent devaluations), which was adopted in the later 1960s, but no clear break with the postwar pattern of unstable economic stagnation is indicated.

The situation in Argentina, Chile, Brazil, Colombia, and Paki-

3. Richard D. Mallon, "Exchange Policy—Argentina," in Papanek (ed.), *Development Policy*, pp. 180–81.

stan has not been very different from that in other countries. Rather inconclusive devaluations and foreign trade reforms took place in the Philippines in 1962 and in India in 1966, with some foreign assistance in each case. In the postwar period, Turkey has gone through several cycles of control and decontrol of imports (by varying quantitative restrictions), as well as a number of *de facto* and *de jure* devaluations. Without being comprehensive, the Pearson Commission[4] tabulated fifteen multilateral operations undertaken between 1957 and 1968 to reschedule the foreign commercial and official debts of particular LDCs that might otherwise go into default. These debt rollovers usually took place under the auspices of international lending consortia, which provided additional aid and postponed the repayment of old debts. The recipient countries sometimes agreed to reform their foreign exchange mechanisms and make internal adjustments, but usually there was little impact other than the avoidance of immediate bankruptcy.

Fortunately economic science need not be this dismal. Taiwan managed to escape the syndrome of heavy financial and foreign trade repression of the early 1950s to achieve self-sustained industrial growth through the 1960s, with the remarkable export performance shown in Table 10-2. The impetus of South Korea's highly successful reforms in 1964–65 (see Chapter 8) has been maintained to the present time. Yet the Taiwanese struggle with inflation in the 1950s was unnecessarily drawn out, as is the liberalization of foreign trade. Even in Korea, the attraction and absorption of large amounts of foreign short-term capital had a somewhat disruptive effect on the process of liberalizing foreign trade and domestic finance. It is by no means clear that the Koreans have escaped permanently from economic repression.

In this chapter, therefore, three related aspects of the transition problem are analyzed:

—What is inherent in past liberalizations, supported by foreign aid, that makes regression so common?

—How can full liberalization best be accomplished?

—How should flexibility in the foreign exchanges be reconciled with higher domestic interest rates so that flows of foreign short-term capital are used efficiently?

4. Lester B. Pearson, *Partners in Development*, Report of the Commission on International Development (Praeger, 1969), p. 379.

## *Pitfalls in Partial Liberalization with Foreign Capital: The Alpha Economy*

To illustrate, a paradigm will be constructed of a typical economy, "Alpha," which is undergoing incomplete and ultimately unsuccessful liberalization—as have many Asian and Latin American countries. The paradigm does not cover the great diversity of cyclical experience of all LDCs, but it is intended to portray certain common elements in that experience as they impinge on foreign trade and the use of foreign capital.

Suppose Alpha has experienced inflation, so that the exchange rate—as pegged by the central bank—has become overvalued *despite* the "normal" high tariffs and other import quotas of long standing, which protect domestic manufacturing. Relative to the reserves held by the central bank, there is now excess demand for foreign exchange resulting from increased imports (which are now cheaper in domestic currency), a fall off in export earnings as exporters are squeezed by rising internal costs, and a flight of short-term capital as traders begin to anticipate a devaluation. To protect reserves, exchange controls are extended to categories of intermediate products that had hitherto been imported quite freely; and exporters are required to convert their foreign currency earnings back into domestic currency.

Eventually both types of controls force a slowdown in domestic production. Since imports of spare parts, raw materials, subassemblies, and so on, become arbitrarily rationed, a severe supply bottleneck reduces output in sheltered domestic manufacturing. This supply constraint need not be associated with a general decline in profits in this sector, because at least some license-holding industrialists are getting intermediate inputs very cheaply, although not as many as they would like. Exporters, however, are subject to a pure profit squeeze and respond by curtailing production also.

As if an industrial recession was not enough, the flight of capital and the depletion of foreign exchange reserves make it impossible for the government of Alpha to continue to meet normal commercial debts to foreigners—largely credits from foreign suppliers used to import capital goods in the not-so-distant past. A threatened default on long- and short-term foreign loans (official and private) forces a searching examination of domestic policies in consultation with a consortium of international lenders headed by the International Monetary Fund.

Devaluation, an injection of external capital to replenish depleted reserves, and the relaxation of some import restrictions have become inevitable. But how much of each? The IMF is aware that even "normal" tariffs and quotas repress export development and cause the overuse of certain imported materials. Hence, it wants the relaxation of import controls to go considerably beyond removal of those imposed on intermediate goods in the last stages of the crisis. Moreover, to ensure the repayment of any new stabilization loan and rescheduled commercial debts, the IMF wants a devaluation large enough to be sustainable over a prolonged period of time. Besides internal restraints on bank lending and on fiscal deficits, the IMF's recommendations then boil down to removal of a rather wide range of protective tariffs and other quantitative restrictions on imports, a large devaluation, and a limited stabilization loan accompanied by debt rescheduling.

The correct strategy for ending the crisis is seen somewhat differently by the domestic authorities in Alpha. Their main concern is to overcome the industrial stagnation and inflation by restoring the "normal" flow of imported inputs into domestic manufacturing and by reviving exports. The removal of any longstanding tariff and quota protection for domestic manufacturers, which they believe would significantly reduce domestic production incentives, is looked upon with disfavor—possibly to be considered in the future when the crisis is past. Moreover, they are well aware of the implicit subsidies, resulting from the overvalued exchange rate, being received by some consumers and some industrialists who hold import licenses. A large devaluation might upset the economic position of both these groups, besides destabilizing the internal price level. Thus, Alpha's authorities argue for limited liberalization confined mainly to intermediate products and wage goods that have traditionally been imported, a small devaluation, and a large stabilization loan.

A heated debate takes place between the IMF and Alpha's government, possibly with insinuations in the nation's newspapers about the designs that the agents of international capitalism have on Alpha's economy. Finally, a bargain is struck with a moderate devaluation, a sizable loan, and a significant expansion of the "free list" of imports that can enter with, at most, a moderate tariff. Most, though not all, existing domestic manufacturers retain their nearly absolute protection.

With the devaluation and stabilization loan, the exchange rate looks as though it would be stable for at least a year or two, and exporters release inventories and begin new production at more favorable prices. Importers now find it profitable to seek foreign commercial credits because, in the short run, the stability in the exchange rate reduces the expected interest costs (in domestic currency) of using external capital. An increased inflow of direct investment may also be invited by the host government or even made a condition for the stabilization loan by the international consortium. All in all, a sizable amount of foreign capital may be mobilized to finance the expected increase in imports. Inventories of intermediate goods for domestic manufacturing are restocked, the supply bottleneck is released, and output revives. Indeed, the capacity of protected domestic industry may also increase as imports of capital goods enter, along with current inputs.

Evidently the "liberalization" and capital inflow have increased the basic distortions in the economy, although the immediate crisis is overcome. Import-competing industries, which already receive extraordinary protection, expand while domestic producers of many intermediate inputs, capital goods, and even some wage goods continue to be unprotected. The moderate devaluation hardly compensates for foreign-financed inflows of competitive imports in the decontrolled categories in the short run and for the bias of differential import restrictions in the long run. Exporters receive a short-term fillip from the devaluation, but the longer-term anti-protection implicit in continued import restrictions[5] weighs heavily on them as well. It is not surprising, therefore, that export earnings fail to rise sufficiently to permit the high level of imports to continue once the immediate capital inflow slackens. This foreign exchange "constraint" may be further exacerbated by continued inflation at the new (devalued) exchange rate. Regression to more controls and a new crisis seems likely.

The conflict between the IMF and the local authorities under-

5. Because of the symmetry between import and export restrictions in their ultimate impact on domestic resource allocation. (See Chapter 10.)

lines the difficulties inherent in *partial* or *narrow* liberalization. Policymakers in Alpha are aware that placing certain imports on the free list may destroy viable domestic firms that produce competitive products. Extensive import restrictions and extraordinary capital inflows cause foreign exchange and supplier credits in the few liberalized categories to appear excessively cheap. Even the most efficient domestic industries, possibly potential exporters, may not be able to withstand this highly subsidized competition. Domestic unemployment may be aggravated. Hence, national authorities may be quite correct in opposing, *at the margin,* an expansion of the free list to any imports that compete with goods produced domestically.

Put another way, it is likely to be a mistake to identify mature domestic firms (or those best able to withstand international competition) and remove their protection first, while backward industries and "infants" retain the full panoply of protective controls. Social justice hardly requires sacrificing the efficient for the inefficient. Hence, a compromise solution, falling between general liberalization as promoted by the IMF and liberalization that is confined to "essentials," as defined by authorities in Alpha, may ultimately be worse than either extreme. The deleterious protection and antiprotection of such compromised or partial liberalizations can be further accentuated by an extraordinary inflow of foreign capital.

## *Full Liberalization without Foreign Capital: The Beta Economy*

Let us construct another paradigm that is not so painfully realistic. Suppose a political consensus is reached in country Beta to liberalize completely policies that had previously been repressive. Authorities plan to raise real interest rates and expand organized finance to its optimum, as described in Chapter 9; and they plan a transition to a neutral foreign trade and tax policy, as was described in Chapter 10. The collection of internal price controls, tax-subsidy combinations, and rationing is to be withdrawn as inflation is brought under control.

The planning problem in Beta then is not whether, or how much, to liberalize, but rather how to coordinate the various phases of a thorough liberalization program. Moreover, policymakers in Beta proceed on their own volition without waiting for an extreme crisis that depletes exchange reserves and throws the country into the arms of external creditors.

Unlike Alpha's reliance on foreign capital, the initial focus is on Beta's *internal* financial constraint. The government moves to increase its own saving by raising taxes and the prices of publicly dispensed services so as to reduce fiscal dependence on credit from the central bank. At the same time, interest rates on deposits and loans are increased in order to stimulate the flow of private savings through organized banking. The initial sharp rise in nominal rates of interest reflects actual inflation and inflationary expectations, and nominal (but not real) rates of interest are reduced as inflation slackens. Eliminating the monetary constraint on internal capital accumulation, through raising the real interest rate on deposits and stimulating investment of higher productivity, maintains the level of output and employment. The fundamental complementarity between real money and new investment, as illustrated in Chapter 8 by the Korean financial reform, is fully exploited by Beta in the course of its price stabilization program.

The release of the internal financial bottleneck simplifies and changes the optimum strategy for liberalizing foreign trade in Beta as compared to Alpha. Authorities in Beta now feel free to reduce restrictions across all import categories *evenly,* with the ultimate objective of removing them entirely. Selective liberalization for some imports where "free lists" are distinguished from "prohibited lists" is avoided, along with the attendant risk of selective demolition of viable enterprises. In Alpha, on the other hand, authorities felt forced to retain at least some trade restrictions for influencing resource allocation because of the absence of a functioning capital market.

As long as all import-substitution industries in Beta have their formal protection lowered simultaneously, the compensating devaluation[6] in the foreign exchanges ensures that no single producer faces unduly harsh or subsidized competition. Antiprotection

6. An uneasy case for prolonging the period over which the devaluation takes place is made in the next section without affecting any major conclusions reached here under the assumption of a discrete devaluation.

for particular industries relative to their position under free trade is thereby avoided. Equity and efficiency are preserved both in appearance and in fact. Moreover, the general devaluation interacts with the liberalized domestic financial system to permit a rapid growth of export and other previously negatively protected industries, which now face higher foreign and domestic prices relative to their production costs. In a microeconomic sense, protective tariffs and exclusive import licenses can no longer be justified as a means for allocating "capital" in the mode of the intervention syndrome analyzed in Chapter 3.

From an aggregative point of view, not only should imports be widely spread, but their total volume should be limited to a normal flow, governed mainly by export earnings. The liberalization of restraints on importing need not mean an immediate increase in imports. Significant domestic unemployment (resulting from a fall in aggregate production) can be avoided if increases in aggregate imports are matched by increases in aggregate exports. A flexible or freely floating exchange rate (with an initial substantial devaluation) is probably necessary at first to ensure that the two are matched as the initial shock of liberalization takes hold. In this way, the economy has an immediate reallocation problem but no need to slacken overall resource use. If there is any fall in production in import substitution industries (and, because of a growth in the production of industrial intermediate goods, there may well not be any fall), balanced trade ensures an offsetting expansion of production for export.

But there may be clouds on the horizon. The delicate internal employment reallocation within Beta may be upset by an unusually large inflow of foreign capital that inhibits the exchange rate from depreciating sufficiently. Aggregate imports then would rise above exports so that the tradable goods sector as a whole would be negatively protected. (Indeed, an import surplus is the real embodiment of a capital inflow.) Previously protected import-competing industries, which face a significant adjustment problem anyway, could have their difficulties magnified by the unusual inflow of competitive imports—say, manufactured consumer goods—that was not directly offset by an increase in domestic demand. Hence, the capital inflow could trigger a decline in overall domestic output because an increase in the production of exportables need no longer counterbalance a reduced production of import-ables. Thus, as it liberalizes, Beta deliberately avoids an unusual or extraordinary injection of foreign capital, whether of stabiliza-tion loans or supplier credits. Hence, Beta also avoids an acute repayment problem with all its attendant pressure to regress on the trade liberalization at a later stage.

What a paradoxical reversal in the role of foreign capital in-flows! In Alpha, external financial support was necessary to rebuild exchange reserves, to provide vital inputs for industrial expansion, and possibly to reduce the government's fiscal dependence on the issue of nominal money. In Beta, extraordinary foreign capital in-flows are viewed with a jaundiced eye on the grounds that they complicate the adjustment to free trade, which could otherwise be adequately handled by the liberalized domestic capital market.

The moral seems clear enough. Without internal financial or fiscal liberalization and with depleted exchange reserves, foreign capital may be necessary to end a crisis and underwrite partial liberalization. But there is an inherent contradiction in the use of foreign capital to secure the *full* liberalization of foreign trade, because capital inflows themselves may inhibit the complete re-moval of import restrictions during the liberalization and its after-math.

## Misaligned Interest Rates and Capital Inflows: Korea Again

The appropriate use of foreign capital can be more easily de-scribed than controlled. This control problem goes beyond simply deciding whether or not to accept official loans or grants-in-aid from abroad. Private incentives to move capital through the for-eign exchanges can be enormous during the liberalization process. Sharp increases in rates of interest on domestic assets, the dis-mantling of detailed foreign exchange restrictions, and significant actual and expected changes in the price of foreign currency can cause large and possibly perverse capital flows.

The analysis here concentrates on *short-term* capital movements —especially trade credit—in the context of an idealized Beta-type liberalization and the somewhat less pure liberalization occurring in Korea. The situation facing an economy *after* a major discrete devaluation and movement toward financial liberalization is analyzed below.

A sharp rise in domestic nominal rates of interest, and the expectation of exchange rate stability in the near term, increases the propensity of nationals—exporters for example—to hold bank deposits in Beta's currency instead of in foreign currencies. (The acquisition by foreigners of bank deposits in Beta may also increase, but is more amenable to direct regulation by Beta's central bank.) In the long run, this willingness to hold bank deposits in Beta helps to avoid unwanted capital flight, once complex exchange controls, rules on export retentions, and so on are removed. Fortunately Swiss bank accounts bearing interest of 2 or 3 percent a year are no longer important to any but the most secretive of Beta's citizens. Financial reform ends the chronic dissipation of Beta's savings in low-return foreign investments and makes it easier for the government to decontrol the foreign exchanges. At the same time, exporters will be free to grant the customary thirty- to ninety-day commercial credit, although high domestic interest rates may provide too great an incentive to factor accounts receivable abroad.

Potentially high and variable trade credit on the import side, however, seems far more likely to be a source of destabilizing capital *inflows,* in the short run during the economic destabilization, despite Beta's history of chronic capital flight. Advanced nations have ample credit facilities, and standard thirty- to ninety-day financing for exports of consumer goods or current industrial inputs to Beta could easily be extended to six months. More important, perhaps, official guarantees by advanced countries on longer-term supplier credits—one to five years—for exports of machinery and other equipment to the less developed countries (LDCs) have grown to quite massive proportions.[7] Individual exporters in the

7. The OECD estimates that the *net* flow of these guaranteed one-to-five-year credits into all LDCs amounted to about $2.7 billion in 1970—about the same order of magnitude as the net inflow of private direct investment. Correspondingly, gross flows were much greater, amounting to about $6.7 billion. Somewhat surprisingly, nonguaranteed private export credits, of this one-to-five-year duration, amounted to only about $64 million net. Hence, only a small proportion of longer-term export credits were subject to normal commercial risk or evaluation. Edwin M. Martin, *Development Assistance, 1971 Review* (Paris: Organisation for Economic Co-operation and Development, 1971), pp. 96, 170.

advanced countries feel no personal commercial risk in concentrating such flows over a short period of time because their own government is providing the guarantee. Hence, for any single LDC, the concentration of these guaranteed credits, plus very short-term commercial credits, can be huge in any given year.

The Korean reforms of 1964–65 are instructive in this respect, although their liberalization of foreign trade was not as broadly based as in the fictitious Beta experiment. Korea devaluated its currency substantially in moving from a multiple exchange-rate system, where the principal import rate was 130 *won* to the dollar until May 1964, to a unified rate of 270 *won* to the dollar by May 1965. At the same time, nominal rates of interest on certain classes of time deposits were increased by as much as 15 percentage points, to a maximum of 30 percent in September 1965—with a substantial increase in most bank lending rates to a "standard" level of 26 percent. These reforms, plus some increases in government saving, dampened inflation and permitted exports and real output to expand rapidly, as was described in Chapter 8. By 1966 the newly devalued exchange rate looked as if it would be stable for some time.

The incentives to move funds into Korea in one form or another had become enormous. The high *nominal* domestic interest rates looked like high *real* rates to foreigners, who had the option of repatriating short-term investments at a stable foreign exchange parity. To most domestic savers, however, the alternative to holding bank deposits was to hold physical commodities as a means of hedging against inflation. International traders, on the other hand, did have the option of holding or borrowing foreign exchange. For example, foreign supplier credits bearing an interest rate in dollars of only 6 percent looked very cheap to Korean importers, who might have to borrow at 26 percent domestically for repayment in *won*—as long as the price of foreign exchange was expected to remain stable. In a fundamental sense, real interest rates seen by "foreigners" investing in Korea had become misaligned with, and higher than, those seen by most Koreans because the stable exchange rate did not reflect expectations of future inflation in the *won* prices of commodities.

An explosive inflow of short- and intermediate-term private capital began in late 1966. The Korean "short-term" debt (with original maturity of less than three years) increased from virtually nothing in 1962 to $70 million by the end of 1966, and to $343 million by the end of 1968 (as estimated by Gilbert Brown), which was close to 40 percent of the value of Korean foreign exchange earnings.[8] Most of this was trade credit for imports, with longer private portfolio capital also being absorbed in significant amounts. This accumulation has become increasingly unstable as repayment worries mount in the early 1970s.

What immediate problems did this capital inflow pose for the Korean authorities? The exchange rate—although nominally free to float—had remained stable through the first half of 1966. Left to itself in late 1966, the *won* would have appreciated sharply due to the avalanche of short-term capital, which was supplemented by increasing remittances of foreign exchange from Korean troops in Vietnam. Quite correctly, the authorities did not want to jeopardize the expansion of their exports of manufactured goods by a sharp appreciation. This left them with a choice between two difficult courses of action for maintaining the exchange rate at 270, other than taking direct measures to restrict capital inflows. Either the central bank had to enter the foreign exchange market and buy dollars by selling *won*, or the minister of commerce and industry could complete the liberalization of imports by removing the strict quota protection enjoyed by domestic manufacturers of import substitutes. Increased imports would then soak up the dollar inflow. The Korean government chose the former course, however, and began rapidly accumulating large dollar reserves.

Before exploring the monetary consequences of this reserve accumulation, it is worthwhile to look at the pressure that was placed on Korean authorities (contrary to the advice of official international agencies) *not* to opt for broader-based import liberalization. Although the *won* had been devalued substantially so as to ameliorate the effects of removing quota restrictions that protected import substitutes, competitive foreign imports could still have entered in unusually large amounts because of the overabundance of cheap trade credit. The misalignment of real interest rates seen by foreign, as compared to domestic, manufacturers may well have

8. From the typed manuscript of a forthcoming book tentatively entitled "Pricing Policies and Economic Development: Korea in the 1960s," Chap. 8, p. 3.

placed the latter at a competitive disadvantage. Of course, political pressure from the protected industries was intense, but it is not unrealistic to suppose that this overabundance of foreign exchange was an important factor in inhibiting—by a narrow margin—a much broader import liberalization in 1967 than Korea actually undertook. Moreover, a low subsidized credit rate of 6.5 to 7 percent for exporters was deemed necessary to maintain export competitiveness. In short, a full Beta-type liberalization of foreign trade and finance was impeded despite an otherwise successful economic policy.

Unfortunately, the accumulation of dollar reserves in lieu of import liberalization had unforeseen consequences. After the financial and fiscal reforms of 1965, the central bank secured control for a short while over the issue of nominal money, and the wholesale price level was actually stabilized through the last two quarters of 1965 and the first quarter of 1966—a substantial achievement in view of Korea's earlier proclivity toward inflation. But because the Bank of Korea was forced to buy dollars from the capital inflow in the last half of 1966, it had to sell "high powered" *won* to the domestic banking system and hence lost control over the creation of nominal money.[9] Gilbert Brown and Edward Shaw have both related the excess issue of nominal money beyond the real demand for money to the accumulation of foreign exchange reserves. Whether one attributes this accumulation primarily to short-term capital inflows, or to the remittances resulting from the U.S. financing of Korean troops in Vietnam, makes no difference.

Price inflation, at a more moderate rate than before 1965, returned by mid-1966. The rise in the wholesale price index (WPI), with the exchange rate fixed at 270, inhibited import liberalization even more; and the interval over which the Korean government has had to maintain high nominal rates of interest to offset the inflation was prolonged. Moreover, the cumulative effect of inflation eventually caused the exchange rate to be overvalued vis-à-vis the large overhang of short-term indebtedness to foreigners. Ad-

9. The lack of a primary securities market in Korea inhibited the central bank from using open market operations to mop up the excess bank reserves created. Even so, such sales of government securities would have redoubled the pressure for foreign capital inflows.

verse speculation eventually forced a major devaluation of the *won* in June 1971 to 370 to the U.S. dollar.[10] Clearly, foreign capital flows and other remittances have created problems for the Korean authorities. It is by no means clear that Korea can absorb short-term capital efficiently as long as "real" rates of interest from the point of view of foreigners differ from those seen by domestic nationals.

## Optimal Monetary Policy and a Gliding Foreign Exchange Parity

Given their innovative moves to liberalize foreign trade and domestic finance, the Korean authorities should not be faulted *ex post* for their foreign exchange policy. With the benefit of hindsight, let us investigate how the exchange rate might optimally be controlled in the course of a full Beta-type liberalization—similar to, but more complete than, that experienced by Korea. The critical problem is to ensure that real rates of interest as seen by foreigners and by domestic nationals are more closely aligned. The opportunity costs of using foreign capital are then weighed more accurately, and, what is most important, domestic control over the supply of nominal money is not upset by large short-term capital inflows after liberalization begins.

Although nominal rates of interest are raised sharply at first, they should gradually be reduced as actual and anticipated inflation in the WPI slackens.[11] To help maintain external balance, however, there is a case for also having the foreign exchange rate depreciate slowly in a predictable way after the initial surprise devaluation. Instead of devaluing fully to "the" equilibrium exchange rate associated with free trade, suppose the authorities undertake a somewhat smaller discrete devaluation. Initially, trade

10. There had been some minor devaluations between 1965 and 1971, when Korea was nominally without an officially determined foreign exchange parity. *De facto*, the government always played a major role in determining what the rate actually was—as most governments are forced to do.

11. The reasons for using the WPI instead of the consumer price index (CPI) or some other price index were given in Chapter 8. The experience of Taiwan, Korea, and Indonesia in reducing nominal interest rates as inflationary expectations were dampened was also discussed.

restrictions are evenly relaxed, although not removed entirely. Then the exchange rate begins to depreciate *smoothly,* at an annual percentage rate that reflects the difference between foreign and domestic nominal rates of interest—with a suitable risk premium subtracted from the latter. A large inflow of foreign short-term capital is avoided because users and lenders of foreign short-term capital (trade credit) take the continuing depreciation into account. (The adjustment period for domestic industries that are losing protection can also be stretched out.)

For example, suppose import credit is available at 6 percent in terms of dollars. The equivalent domestic loan in Beta's currency initially carries a nominal interest rate of 20 percent immediately after reform occurs. However, the government announces that it expects Beta's currency to depreciate evenly over the course of the year by 10 percent—at a rate of about 0.2 percent a week or other amounts so small that speculators have nothing to gain by anticipating the changes. Then the effective cost of using foreign supplier credits denominated in dollars will rise by about 10 percentage points to approximately 16 percent—about equivalent to borrowing costs in Beta once a realistic risk premium is taken into account. Large inward movements of foreign short-term capital can then be dampened substantially, and the central bank will maintain control over the money supply by preventing an untoward buildup of exchange reserves. Growth in short-term indebtedness to foreigners will be avoided.

Postponing a portion of the total required adjustment has the further advantage of avoiding windfall gains to some exporters before additional production for export is actually generated. The future, more favorable price of foreign exchange can be anticipated by announcing the rate at which the parity glides downward. The elasticity of response by exporters in the future would be increased by the release of such information. Correspondingly, many import-substitution industries would have more time to prepare for the bracing wind of international competition.

There is an extensive literature on the gliding parity,[12] which is

---

12. The first contribution probably was John H. Williamson's *The Crawling Peg,* Essays in International Finance, No. 50 (Princeton University, International Finance Section, 1965). The demerits of the rather squalid crawling peg or merits of the more elegant gliding parity have been extensively discussed in the Princeton series, mainly in the context of advanced industrial economies.

too lengthy to review here. A gradual exchange rate devaluation has been used with considerable success by the Brazilian government since 1968 and was also used by Chile until the experiment was ended by the Allende government in 1970. Our principal concern, however, is the conscious use of the downward gliding parity as an instrument of domestic monetary control[13] in the immediate aftermath of a major liberalization. If the reforms are successful in halting inflation, the downward glide might end after one or two years when domestic nominal rates of interest are reduced. Otherwise, the gliding parity can be used residually as an international balancing device in both commodity and financial markets if inflation continues.

## On Restricting Inflows of Short-Term Capital

The gliding parity, for aligning foreign and domestic interest rates during liberalization, may well prove too delicate for many governments to handle. The division of exchange-rate adjustment between the initial discrete devaluation and the magnitude and duration of the smooth downward glide to follow has to be carefully calculated. Both the degree to which foreign trade had been repressed and the speed with which inflationary expectations are to be dampened would enter into this determination, as would changes in nominal rates of interest. The even dismantling of import restrictions then has to be matched to the projected speed of the moving exchange rate. All in all, the basis for deciding which is the most efficient procedure for using the gliding parity is complicated—both conceptually and empirically—and planned procedures would have to be applied with some care.

During liberalization, however, the case for restricting the use of foreign short-term capital—particularly supplier credits for imports—may be quite strong as a supplement to exchange rate policy. At the very least, LDCs can dismantle official regulatory devices set up for the express purpose of encouraging the use of

13. A more complete theoretical analysis, apart from the liberalization question, is provided in Ronald I. McKinnon, *Monetary Theory and Controlled Flexibility in the Foreign Exchanges*, Essays in International Finance, No. 84 (Princeton University, International Finance Section, 1971).

foreign short-term finance. Advance deposit requirements for imports, licenses to import, and complementary domestic import finance are often geared to the amount of foreign credit that potential domestic importers can negotiate. Indeed, in poor economies, strong incentives to draw on foreign sources of finance are hardly surprising, even though the composition of imports may be badly distorted by easy credit terms. Special incentives to import capital should be abolished permanently, along with tariff and quota restrictions on commodity trade.

Reform-minded governments may want to go further, however. A really widespread liberalization in foreign trade (including consumer goods) and finance, associated with a large discrete devaluation and a sharp rise in rates of interest, can make temporary administrative restraint over short-term inflows of foreign capital a virtual necessity. Besides rejecting stabilization loans and other extraordinary government-to-government aid, the authorities may restrict the purchase of domestic financial assets by foreigners and sharply limit the trade credit that importers are permitted to accept. Even so, the administrative problems of distinguishing "normal" from "abnormal" commercial credits on imports are formidable and are made even more so by various insurance programs for export credits on the part of advanced countries, which blur normal commercial distinctions. Fortunately, the need for, and desirability of, such extraordinary measures will fade as financial liberalization dampens domestic inflationary expectations, and domestic nominal rates of interest can be reduced.

The basic paradox remains, however. Despite conventional wisdom, foreign capital need not be necessary to provide critical leverage in the liberalization process. On the contrary, there are circumstances where its use should be deliberately rejected.

# 12

## Some Concluding Notes on Inflows of Foreign Capital

THIS BOOK HAS BEEN devoted largely to the role of capital and capital markets in poor countries. However, it has not yet investigated government-to-government aid transfers or the direct investments of giant multinational corporations in their subsidiaries in the developing countries. Moreover, officially guaranteed export credits from advanced countries—another form of "development assistance," as classified by the Organisation for Economic Co-operation and Development (OECD)—were shown in Chapter 11 to be potential impediments to liberalization, as well as having other unfortunate characteristics. Evidently the transfer of capital from wealthy countries to less developed countries (LDCs) is being given a lower priority and a different status from that accorded by aid-giving agencies or even laissez-faire economists who have dreams of restoring the great international capital market as it operated before 1914.

This anomalous status of international capital flows reflects the basic theme of this book. Financial repression restrains domestic saving within LDCs and generates pressure for reliance on foreign capital to supplement domestic saving and to provide intermediation services capable of identifying high-return investment opportunities that would otherwise languish. Similarly, the repression of foreign trade inhibits the development of exports and creates an apparent "shortage" of foreign exchange that ostensibly can also be relieved by inflows of foreign capital. In the repressed economies, therefore, foreign loans or grants play the important dual role of relaxing the saving constraint on the one hand and the foreign exchange constraint on the other. (One could go further and identify a third constraint, a fiscal one, that requires soliciting budgetary support from abroad because the government cannot raise revenue domestically.) There is now an extensive literature on the impact on growth of foreign capital inflows, assuming that either a savings or a foreign exchange constraint is binding.[1] Repression is implicitly being taken for granted.

Experience suggests, however, that foreign funds may be managed no more rationally than funds of domestic origin. When they are loaned, the rates of interest often bear no relationship to the scarcity price of capital. The enclave syndrome, discussed in Chapter 2, can easily be aggravated. Returns actually repatriated by foreigners may be at great variance with their correctly measured economic contribution. Governments become accustomed to foreign aid for their own fiscal support on current and capital account and feel less need for "organized" financial processes for allocating capital on a decentralized basis at much higher rates of interest.

Similarly the foreign exchange constraint can be exacerbated by undue reliance on foreign capital. A disequilibrium exchange rate, where exporters are punished by the low official price of foreign currency, is more easily maintained if minimal imports are supplied by a foreign aid program—even one administered on a multilateral basis. Inflation may be tolerated a little longer before devaluation occurs.[2] Domestic industry can become overly depen-

1. See, for example, Hollis B. Chenery and Alan M. Strout, "Foreign Assistance and Economic Development," *American Economic Review*, Vol. 56 (September 1966), pp. 679–733; and Ronald I. McKinnon, "Foreign Exchange Constraints in Economic Development and Efficient Aid Allocation," *Economic Journal*, Vol. 74 (June 1964), pp. 388–409.

2. Benjamin I. Cohen, in "Relative Effects of Foreign Capital and Larger Exports on Economic Development," *Review of Economics and Statistics*, Vol. 50 (May 1968), pp. 281–84, has correlated the total inflows of capital (mainly governmental) in a number of underdeveloped countries with their export performance and growth in gross national product. In aggregate terms, the period 1955–60 was one of fairly rapid expansion in net aid and also one of export stagnation for underdeveloped economies in twenty-seven LDCs. The period 1960–65 (forty-one countries) was one in which the net level of aid stagnated while exports grew considerably faster than in the previous period. Going further within each period, Cohen finds a slight negative correlation between net capital inflows and export expansion for a cross-section of the LDCs.

dent on imported industrial materials and capital goods, which are unduly cheap in terms of the domestic currency, and which are pushed heavily by mercantile interests in the exporting countries.

Clearly, the preferred strategy is to liberalize domestic finance and foreign trade directly rather than to rely on foreign capital to alleviate chronic "bottlenecks." It would be unfair, however, to criticize existing programs of development assistance on the assumption that most LDCs are about to liberalize. That would be wishful thinking. But it would be equally inappropriate for donor countries and multinational agencies to accept fiscal and financial repression as a given, if regrettable, state of affairs. Liberalization is a real possibility to be encouraged, as was seen in Chapter 11.

## Foreign Direct Investment: Were the Japanese Right?

Assuming benign tolerance by advanced countries, in what direction might policy evolve within the LDCs that are successfully liberalizing? The historic role of multinational corporations in the third world began with the export enclaves, and in many poor countries they have come to dominate fledgling domestic manufacturing of import substitutes. Yet this is neither an inevitable nor necessarily efficient pattern of development. Indeed, the basic theoretical approach of this book suggests that distortions in factor markets cause over-use of foreign sources of finance in a way that may well have emasculated domestic entrepreneurial growth. (See Chapter 3.) Correspondingly, the bootstrap theory here implies that reliance on foreign direct investment—with its package of finance, modern technology, and managerial skills—should be curtailed by LDCs themselves in order to promote balanced indigenous development.

In the absence of historical precedent, one might well be suspicious of such a sweeping conclusion. Fortunately Japan provides an excellent example of a poor economy that had a liberal foreign trade policy forced on it by gun-boat diplomacy. That is, trade in the current account of the balance of payments was virtually free from 1870, when the Meji restoration initiated "modern" Japanese development, to the turn of the century. Rather than relying on foreign sources of finance, however, Japan developed its own

TABLE 12-1. *Aggregate Value of Foreign Direct Investment and Net Inflow, Seven Major Industrial Countries, Various Dates, 1960–66*
Millions of U.S. dollars

| Country | Aggregate amount, 1964 | Net inflow, 1960–66 |
|---|---|---|
| Canada | 14,500[a] | 3,404 |
| France | 4,000 | 1,440 |
| Germany | 2,784 | 2,507 |
| Italy | n.a. | 2,438 |
| Japan | 400[b] to 725[c] | 409 |
| United Kingdom | 4,200[a] | 3,461 |
| United States | 8,363[d] | 2,350 |

Source: Organisation for Economic Co-operation and Development, *Liberalisation of International Capital Movements: Japan* (Paris: OECD, 1968), Table 1.
    a. 1962 for Canada; end of 1962 for United Kingdom.
    b. Official Japanese estimate for mid-1965.
    c. Unofficial OECD estimate for mid-1965.
    d. End of year.
    n. a. = Not available.

efficient financial system in the late nineteenth century while it was still poor. Indeed, Hugh T. Patrick[3] has interpreted Japanese growth as being induced by the creation of a modern banking system in the 1870s and by the opening of the economy to foreign trade in the 1850s. Japanese banking was, and is, a "leading sector."

From the start of its open development, foreign direct investment in Japan was inhibited by cultural differences, the competitiveness of domestic finance, and by official policies. Consequently even today the book value of business enterprises that are controlled by foreigners is much less in Japan than in other industrial countries. (See Table 12-1.) The estimate of $400 million to $700 million for foreign investments in Japan in 1965 is an order of magnitude smaller than the $10 billion to $13 billion of foreign direct investments in Latin America, whose aggregate gross national product was then of comparable size.

While the Japanese have deliberately restricted foreign ownership and managerial control, they have relied on inflows of portfolio capital in certain critical periods in their history associated with wars, although not in the formative stage before 1897, when

3. "Financial Development and Economic Growth in Underdeveloped Countries," *Economic Development and Cultural Change*, Vol. 14 (January 1966), pp. 177, 180.

the gold standard was adopted.[4] The Japanese repayment record is impeccable, due in part to careful official scrutiny of new obligations.

More important, Japan has succeeded in separating the importation of foreign technology from the acceptance of foreign direct investment. In the late nineteenth and early twentieth centuries, much of this separation was carried out by unrequited copying of foreign goods and industrial processes. By the 1920s, however, it began to be systematized through the formal purchases of foreign patents, licensing agreements, and joint ventures between Japanese and foreign companies with superior technologies. Well financed local entrepreneurs or the government almost always retained complete managerial control over manufacturing in Japan. Concomitantly, the service charges for foreign patent and licensing rights bulk large as a current outflow in the Japanese balance of payments.

To be sure, economic growth in poor countries may be slowed in the short run if access to the highly proficient multinational corporations is foreclosed. Even in the long run, growth may be slowed if foreign corporations are not retained for a few highly specialized and risky tasks, such as off-shore drilling for petroleum, which are simply too expensive for the host country to undertake. Nevertheless, the use of the multinational corporation as the main vehicle for absorbing modern technology and managerial skills seems unlikely to be consistent with broadly based domestic entrepreneurial and financial development. It is difficult to see how the enclave syndrome can be avoided when such large corporations operate in a markedly different cultural environment.

## Investment and Credit Guarantees by Wealthy Countries

Although the Japanese consciously rejected direct investment by foreigners in their own formative years, Japanese nationals are now being encouraged to invest in poorer countries and to retain man-

4. For a more detailed discussion, see Saburo Okita and Takeo Miki, "Treatment of Foreign Capital—A Case Study for Japan," in John H. Adler (ed.), *Capital Movements and Economic Development,* Proceedings of a Conference held by the International Economics Association (Macmillan, 1967), pp. 139–68.

agerial control of these investments. But the Japanese are not alone. Recent reductions in government-to-government loans by the United States have been associated with efforts to spur direct U.S. investments in LDCs.

The United States Overseas Private Investment Corporation (OPIC) was formed in 1970 to extend and significantly increase public insurance of private U.S. direct investments in less developed countries. The traditional specific-risk insurance on noncommercial hazards in the form of currency inconvertibility, expropriation, insurrection, and so on, is to be augmented by OPIC to cover most American corporations operating in LDCs. "It is now estimated that insurance is purchased for about two-thirds of new and eligible United States investments."[5] In addition, an increasing proportion of purely commercial risk—not due to outright fraud or misconduct—is to be covered. Private equity investments, including supporting bank loans and bond issues, are underwritten and encouraged by OPIC. The OECD review mentions a number of similar financial institutions that have been set up by major European countries, as part of their development assistance efforts, to bail out private nationals whose property is expropriated or who suffer commercial losses in poor countries. Commercial and noncommercial losses are not readily distinguishable in highly repressed economies.

Aside from the evident mercantilist motivations of the advanced countries, what are the implications of such investment guarantees in recipient LDCs? Perhaps the concealment of normal commercial risk is inherent in a highly repressed and unstable economic environment. Still, an important reason for using foreign financial services is to distinguish between good and poor investments, viable and nonviable enterprise, and so on. This *raison d'être* may well be lost under generalized insurance, which implicitly assumes that all capital is equally productive, in striking contrast to the fragmentation hypothesis developed in Chapter 2. That is, poor investments are all too prevalent in the less developed countries; and public insurance programs may simply increase the likelihood that more low-return projects are undertaken. Capital is not uniformly productive.

5. Edwin M. Martin, *Development Assistance, 1970 Review* (Paris: Organisation for Economic Co-operation and Development, 1971), p. 85.

Countries with repressed economies may find that "insured" direct investments by foreigners, like guaranteed supplier credits on imports, are not to their advantage over the long run. In liberalized economies, on the other hand, such programs may well be redundant if the developing countries choose to follow the early Japanese model, where direct foreign managerial control played no significant role but unrepressed domestic finance was heavily utilized.

For advanced countries, then, a case can be made for the multilateral elimination of generalized insurance guarantees on capital flows to poor countries, much like the case for the untying of bilateral aid. Essentially, OECD countries could agree to confine finance for export supplier credits and for direct investments abroad to "normal" commercial channels without national guarantees. No individual industrial country need lose its commercial position, and governments would no longer feel as much pressure to defend the economic interests of their private citizens.

## Unbiased Absorption of International Capital

Poor countries have been cavalier in their use of foreign capital, although a puritanical approach would have served them better. However, foreign capital can be used efficiently, as can domestic capital, once internal financial machinery is set up (as described in Chapters 6–11) and the foreign exchanges are suitably liberalized (see Chapters 10 and 11). Both reforms have the effect of making domestic money a stable numeraire internationally and could be expected to change fundamentally the way in which capital is best transferred to the liberalized economy in question.

Instead of absorbing capital through aid or unstable inflows of short-run trade credit, or by yielding managerial control, public and private institutions could sell to foreigners longer-term securities—preferred stock, bonds, convertible debentures, and so on —in moderate amounts. The return on some of these securities might be denominated in the domestic currency if the foreign investor were willing to assume the exchange risk as well as the underlying commercial risk; or the bonds might be issued with U.S. dollars as the numeraire so that domestic business firms would now assume the exchange risk. In either case, foreign investors and investment analysts would be concerned with the commercial riskiness of the locally controlled enterprise and its ultimate expected rate of return. Foreigners would also be attracted by high domestic rates of interest, although the problem of properly aligning domestic and foreign real rates of interest would remain a delicate one.

Financial intermediaries—some publicly controlled—could expedite this flow of international portfolio capital by spreading risks and providing information to potential investors within LDCs. Purely national institutions, like Mexico's Nacional Financiera and the Puerto Rican Development Board, could sell their own bonds in New York or London and invest the proceeds domestically. Alternatively, these national institutions might wish to provide *selective* guarantees on debt issues by domestic enterprises— borrowers whose viability and contribution to development had been thoroughly researched. Multilateral lending on "hard" terms by the International Bank for Reconstruction and Development also fits within the framework here for the transmission of international portfolio capital in a liberalized environment.

With a thriving domestic capital market and access to foreign portfolio finance, liberalized LDCs may well contemplate restraints on foreign direct investment and managerial control—particularly when the development of the domestic capital market and entrepreneurial expertise are still in their formative stages. Although these residual restrictions may remain on the capital account of the balance of payments, liberalization would permit completely free trade in goods and services on the current account—again along the lines of the early Japanese experience.

Readers may note that the postwar strategy followed by many LDCs—particularly those in Latin America—has been the obverse of Japan's early strategy. That is, the current account of the balance of payments—imports and exports—has been subject to heavy restrictions while much foreign direct investment has been absorbed through the capital account. Undoubtedly internal financial repression contributed heavily to this unfortunate reversal of what migh be considered an "optimal" foreign exchange policy for a developing economy.

# Index